# REPRESENTATIVE
# AMERICAN SPEECHES
# 1975-1976

**edited by WALDO W. BRADEN**
**Boyd Professor of Speech**
**Louisiana State University**

## THE REFERENCE SHELF
**Volume 48   Number 4**

## THE H. W. WILSON COMPANY
New York   1976

# THE REFERENCE SHELF

The books in this series contain reprints of articles, excerpts from books, and addresses on current issues and social trends in the United States and other countries. There are six separately bound numbers in each volume, all of which are generally published in the same calendar year. One number is a collection of recent speeches; each of the others is devoted to a single subject and gives background information and discussion from various points of view, concluding with a comprehensive bibliography. Books in the series may be purchased individually or on subscription.

Copyright © 1976
By The H. W. Wilson Company
*International Standard Book Number 0-8242-0598-7*

PRINTED IN THE UNITED STATES OF AMERICA

**Library of Congress Catalog Card**
Representative American speeches, 1937/38–
    New York, H. W. Wilson Co.
        v. 21. cm. annual. (The Reference shelf)
    Editors: 1937/38–1958/59, A. C. Baird.—1959/60–1969/70,
        L. Thonssen.—1970/71—    W. W. Braden.

    1. American orations. 2. Speeches, addresses, etc.
I. Baird, Albert Craig, ed.    II. Thonssen, Lester,
ed.        III. Braden, Waldo W., ed.        IV. Series.
PS668.B3                    815.5082                38–27962

# PREFACE

## AN OVERVIEW OF PUBLIC ADDRESS, 1975-1976

What conclusion can one reach about the quality of American public address in the last year? In the language of the wine trade, 1975-1976 was not a "good year." Why? The incentives for eloquence have been missing. Dramatic issues have disappeared. Indignation over Watergate has cooled. The American consumer's concern over the energy shortage has dissipated with the return of supplies of gasoline. Controversy over busing has brought forth violence in the streets and angry rhetoric in public debate, but little in the way of distinguished speaking.

Two events have dominated much of the public speaking during this period: the Bicentennial celebration and, of course, the 1976 political campaign. Several of the speeches included in this collection refer to the Bicentennial and four others draw their message directly from the Declaration of Independence and the American Revolution. But no speaker today has dignified the nation's founding in words that compare with Daniel Webster's speeches of one hundred and fifty years ago: his Plymouth Oration, his Adams and Jefferson address, or his Bunker Hill Monument speeches. The public mood of these days cries out for the inspiration of such eloquence as Webster's, for the visible and vocal leadership of a Franklin D. Roosevelt, an Abraham Lincoln, or a Martin Luther King Jr., but the void remains.

The aftermath of Vietnam and Watergate, together with revelations of corruption, influence peddling, and illegal political funds, contributed greatly to the moods of cynicism and pessimism. "Disassociation and disillusionment now infect almost every aspect of our society," concluded David M. Alpern (*Newsweek*, April 12, 1976). In a recent *Newsweek* survey, only 28 percent of those interviewed said "that

3

they had a great deal of trust in most people" they meet. Pollster George Gallup told an audience at the University of Iowa, January 29, 1976: "Never has there been a time in the forty years since we started the Gallup poll when the American people have been so disillusioned, discouraged and confused about life in this country." Some observers of the national scene, viewing the absence of inspiring leadership, predict that no more than 50 percent of the voters will go to the polls in the coming elections.

A moment of some potential inspiration presented itself on the occasion of the State of the Union Message (January 19, 1976), but President Ford put political matters above the concerns of the heart and spirit and delivered an hour-long message that did no more than set forth a political timetable and the planks on which he intended to campaign. Edmund Muskie's reply on the following night was equally mundane.

Since the beginning of 1976, great amounts of rhetorical energy have gone into the presidential primaries. However, the contestants have been more interested in images than ideas; consequently, they produced little of substance or of broad appeal. One reason for this is that too often it was their passing, often impromptu, remarks that media experts made into convenient thirty-second to five-minute spots for television. Moreover, it is the very pace of the political primary races that makes significant public speaking a rarity. Hurried, three- to four-day trips to key states involving fund-raising breakfasts at airports, news conferences at shopping centers and schools, coffee breaks at the gates of plants, staged question-and-answer sessions before the television camera—such hectic routine for the candidates produced much media exposure but little worth recording in a collection of speeches.

Calling the contests "media events," Howard Flieger (*U.S. News & World Report*, March 22, 1976) reported that in New Hampshire he observed "many more reporters and cameramen than . . . voters at some of the polling places."

Another reporter said, "Any major candidate's campaign day is a lengthening chain" of media exposures "measured in feet of film for network and ideal TV news shows" (Joseph Lelyveld, New York *Times,* March 10, 1976). Tom Wicker of the New York *Times* (March 10, 1976) thought that the contribution of the candidates to public understanding was indeed low. In spite of numerous forums, position papers, news conferences, and what were termed "major speeches," Wicker reported in the New York *Times,* March 19, 1976, "so much of what is being said is actively misleading, demagogic, or nonsensical." There is, indeed, much truth in Arthur Schlesinger Jr.'s observation:

The parties are now heavily engaged in going through the motions expected of them in the year before a presidential election. Candidates are making speeches and scurrying around the country. Activists are holding meetings and arguing about endorsements. The press and television are faithfully playing up these exercises as if some great historic drama were unfolding. But the voters seem to be regarding it all with more than the usual ennui. Why does politics appear so particularly irrelevant on the eve of the two-hundredth anniversary of American independence? (*Wall Street Journal,* December 3, 1975)

Readers might well ask the editor of this book, confronted as he is by a singular dearth of good public address, how he can justify the title "Representative American Speeches" and on what basis he chose the speeches to be included in this volume. Following the lead of the two preceding editors, the present editor of REPRESENTATIVE AMERICAN SPEECHES strives to include speeches that typify, or are examples of, the *superior* public address of a given year, speeches that express significant ideas, are well organized, are presented in efficient and persuasive oral language, and are appealing to their listeners. The selection of speeches is, in the last analysis, the editor's own. No poll is conducted to determine what should be included or which speakers deserve recognition. After consulting with many readers and soliciting their evaluations, the editor assembles the final list of from sixteen to twenty speeches.

There are, of course, factors that he takes into account when considering a speech for inclusion: the importance of the issue presented; the prominence of the speaker; the length of the speech (some speeches are simply too long to include in a book of two hundred pages) ; its worthiness as a model or example for study; its interest to the general reader rather than to the critic of rhetoric; its timelessness (it should not be dated by the subject or internal references) ; its universality of theme (the too partisan or too provincial should be avoided) ; and finally, its language, which should be fresh and not technical.

Currently much of public address is the creation of the professional speech writer (who used to be known as a ghost writer). The editor of this compilation prefers to choose speeches that are products of the speakers themselves, not of their employees (or employers). But, admittedly, many speakers—particularly busy government officials—are too often dependent upon their staffs for research and for the actual writing of their speeches.

Many persons have helped in collecting the speeches and have assisted in supplying material included in this book. The speakers and their secretaries have been most cooperative in providing texts, background material, and biographical data. As always, Clinton Bradford, Stephen Cooper, Francine Merritt, Harold Mixon, Owen Peterson, and Barbara Walsh have made valuable suggestions. I am also indebted to Mary Margaret Roberts of Kansas State College of Pittsburg and to Caroline Wire of the Louisiana State University Library staff for calling my attention to particular speeches. Paula Richardson, Linda Rewerts, Beleta Shambra, and Virginia Steely have cheerfully taken dictation, proofread, and typed the manuscript. I am most appreciative of the help of these persons and many others.

WALDO W. BRADEN

August 1976
Baton Rouge, Louisiana

# CONTENTS

ANSWERS FROM ACADEMIA

A HERO HONORED

# THE BICENTENNIAL: REMEMBERING OUR PAST

## ". . . OUR SACRED HONOR" [1]

### JOHN A. HOWARD [2]

To celebrate the Bicentennial, Rockford College, in Rockford, Illinois, planned its forum lectures around the theme "Posterity Must Judge." The lectures were scheduled throughout the academic year and prominent persons from the academic world were invited to participate. John T. Howard, president of the college, opened the series at the first college convocation, September 10, 1975. Widely sought as an academic speaker, Dr. Howard considered this address one of his most important of the year.

Well aware that many of his youthful listeners thought of the signers of the Declaration of Independence as men in "funny" clothes and had concluded that the eighteenth century language of the Declaration is "stilted and self-conscious," Howard attempted to breathe life into the Document by giving a kinescopic view of what the "earnest oath" and ". . . our sacred honor," meant to Patrick Henry, Thomas Jefferson, John Adams, Gouverneur Morris, James Wilson, George Washington, Alexander Hamilton, and John Jay.

The reader should notice how effectively Howard uses analogy. The speech is based upon comparisons and contrasts of the lives of the men in the eighteenth century who were motivated by "our sacred honor" and the lives of persons today. The persuasion results from making a contemporary listener ashamed of complaining in light of what our colonial forebears endured. He made his point evident when he observed that the "key elements within the colonial conception of honorable conduct" were "self-discipline, self-reliance, respect for the law, respect for private property, all pervaded by unselfish concern for the public good."

The solution that Dr. Howard offered is what one would expect him to present to students in a liberal arts college. In contrast to the prevailing philosophy of "a value-free education," he argues that "our nation must . . . reassert the educational

---

[1] Delivered at the fall convocation, Rockford College, Rockford, Illinois, September 10, 1975. Quoted by permission.
[2] For biographical note, see Appendix.

principle to try to train our people in the requirements of responsible liberty." The lesson that the colonial founders of the nation offered emphasized his point concerning "our sacred honor." Rejecting the pessimism that Andrew Hacker expressed in *The End of the American Era* (Atheneum, 1970), Dr. Howard concluded, "A number of our problems come into focus through contemplating the philosophy and the judgments of the intelligent, courageous, wise and virtuous people who founded this nation in far more difficult circumstances than we face today."

The speech showed that the speaker had read widely and had prepared with great care. From the experiences of the Revolutionary generation, he was able to draw lessons that were meaningful to contemporary listeners. The ten quotations he used suggest his extensive research. His development is easy to follow; his language, impressive. The reader will be interested in learning of the care and effort that Dr. Howard put into the speech. When the editor of this book pressed him, Dr. Howard wrote:

> For the Opening Convocation address, I usually choose the topic at least six months before the event and then set aside articles and quotations that bear on the topic as I encounter them thereafter. I add to that pile thoughts that occur to me from time to time which may be pertinent. For this particular talk I gave myself the pleasure of skimming a number of biographies of key figures of the Revolutionary era.
>
> Several weeks before the Convocation, I usually spend three or four days alone at our vacation cabin roughing out the text and then work for briefer periods making refinements up to the moment of presentation.

Howard is a compelling, direct speaker who relates well to his listeners, giving them the comfortable feeling that "he is trying to make his points known to a friend in his living room." During the past year he has made over twenty addresses to groups off campus, including speeches at St. John's Military Academy, Colorado State University, Culver-Stockton College, and Brigham Young University.

For another of Dr. Howard's convocation speeches, see "The Innovation Mirage" in REPRESENTATIVE AMERICAN SPEECHES, 1970-1971.

"And for the support of this Declaration, with a firm reliance on the protection of divine Providence, we mutually pledge our Lives, our Fortunes and our sacred Honor."

This earnest oath which concludes the Declaration of Independence sounds strange to our ears today. To be sure, we still go through the ritual of making vows in various ceremonies—the pledge of fidelity in taking the oath of public office, the assertion with a hand on the Bible that we will tell the truth, the whole truth and nothing but the truth in court, and the promise to forsake all others until death do us part in the wedding rites—but the news and social statistics suggest that many people do not really take these vows very seriously.

As for pledging one's life and one's fortune and really meaning it, most of us would probably have difficulty identifying any fifty-six living Americans who would seriously volunteer such a commitment despite the fact that the population from which we would choose the fifty-six is almost a hundred times more numerous. Turning to that final phrase. *our sacred Honor*, it is for many a concept from another time and another culture, like binding the feet or entombing a Pharaoh in a pyramid, so remote as to have little personal significance two centuries later.

As we begin this year in which our college will be devoting a number of programs and activities to the Bicentennial observance, perhaps an appropriate starting point is an effort to understand and put into a contemporary context the import of the vow taken by those men who, in signing that document, symbolically and actually established this nation as a sovereign state.

In the first place, the natural tendency to evaluate people and events of the past according to their contemporary counterparts might lead us to suppose that John Hancock and his colleagues of the Second Continental Congress were not much different from the people who serve in Congress today, other than the "funny" clothes they wore and the more impressive vocabulary they used. Well, such a supposition would be grossly in error. A far more apt comparison would be with Alexander Solzhenitsyn, Andrei Sakharov and the dauntless and intelligent group of Russian

scientists and men of letters who, at great risk to themselves and their families, have spoken out forcefully against the tyranny which prevails in their land.

To challenge openly one's own government when it is arrogantly authoritarian and has its police troops deployed in the vicinity is not an act to be undertaken lightly. Just as the courageous voices from behind the Iron Curtain are not impetuous young dissidents who risk only their own safety, the members of the Continental Congress were also men of stature, family men, settled and successful and respected lawyers, merchants, and land owners, who had much to lose, and in many cases lost much.

T. R. Fehrenbach's book, *Greatness To Spare*, is a series of biographical sketches of men who signed the Declaration of Independence. The following is the concluding summary from that book:

> Nine signers died of wounds or hardships during the Revolutionary War.
>
> Five were captured or imprisoned, in some cases with brutal treatment.
>
> The wives, sons and daughters of others were killed, jailed, mistreated, persecuted or left penniless. One was driven from his wife's deathbed and lost all his children.
>
> The houses of twelve signers were burned to the ground. Seventeen lost everything they owned.
>
> Every signer was proscribed as a traitor; every one was hunted. Most were driven into flight; most were at one time or another barred from their families or their homes.
>
> Most were offered immunity, freedom, rewards, their property or the lives and release of loved ones to break their pledged word or to take the King's protection. Their fortunes were forfeit, but their honor was not. No signer defected or changed his stand throughout the darkest hours.

It is cruelly evident that the pledge they made was not just a perfunctory assent to a rhetorical flourish of Thomas Jefferson's pen; it was an earnest commitment entered into by thoughtful, pious and intrepid men.

Let us return now to the last phrase, *our sacred Honor,*

and try to understand what it meant to them. First of all, the term refers to a concept of virtue and the sincere effort to live and act according to that concept. Although the leaders of the American Revolution came from vastly differing backgrounds, they had a remarkable commonality in what they regarded as the components of virtue. Aristocrats and commoners, plantation-owners and city dwellers, members of diverse churches and varying professions, they held similar views about the code of conduct which should guide one's life.

Religion played a dominant part in their personal as well as their political philosophy. One man who has been studying this aspect of Revolutionary times, Reverend Edward Bauman, has developed a series of television presentations entitled "God of Our Fathers," which examines the religious dimensions of the lives of Washington, Adams, Jefferson, Madison, Hamilton, John Jay and others. Washington's public speeches and private correspondence are, like Lincoln's, interwoven with sincere religious supplications. Indeed, most of the leaders of the Revolutionary period made genuine and devout reference to God in their various statements, almost as frequently as some of today's leaders use God's name irreverently and profanely in their daily language.

For example, Patrick Henry listed the principles which guided his life, principles instilled in him by his uncle:

> To be true and just in all my dealings. To bear no malice or hatred in my heart. To keep my hands from picking and stealing. Not to covet other men's goods, but to learn and labor truly to get my own living, and to do my duty in that state of life unto which it shall please God to call me.

John Adams wrote in his diary at the time he began his legal training, "The study and the practice of law, I am sure, does not dissolve the obligations of morality and religion."

Such comments, in our era of cynicism, may sound

stilted and self-conscious and self-righteous, but in those days the cultivation and the preservation of character was a paramount goal of both religious and secular education, accepted and fervently supported by most of the leadership of the society. Alexander Hamilton reflects this orthodoxy in a letter to his friend, Edward Stevens. Having had to go to work at the age of eleven, he hoped for better things than he found in his modest job at an accounting firm. "I contemn the groveling existence of a clerk," he wrote, "and would willingly risk my life, though not my character, to exalt my station."

The concern for righteous conduct was even embodied in the Virginia Bill of Rights adopted by the Virginia Assembly in June of 1776. Included was the statement: "No free government or the blessing of liberty can be preserved to any people but by a firm adherence to justice, moderation, temperance, frugality and virtue."

Gouverneur Morris, one of New York's foremost statesmen, and a representative of his state in the Second Continental Congress, is depicted in a biography by Theodore Roosevelt as a veritable tiger of moral principle. "He was absolutely upright and truthful: the least suggestion of falsehood was abhorrent to him . . . and he made open war on all the traits that displeased him, especially meanness and hypocrisy." Early in his career he led the opposition to a bill in the New York Assembly which proposed to meet the heavy costs of the Indian Wars by issuing interest-bearing bonds. Morris vigorously chastised the proponents of the plan for what he called their "criminal and selfish dishonesty in trying to procure a temporary benefit for themselves at the lasting expense of the community." One is moved to lament the absence of a latter-day Gouverneur Morris whose sharp sense of right and wrong might have prevented the massive and unmanageable public debt which has provoked such a towering crisis today in his native city of New York.

The lively concern for moral conduct was quite widely

applied to economic matters as well as personal and political ones. Respect for private property was regarded as one of the basic elements of righteousness. James Wilson, another signer of the Declaration of Independence and one of the original members of the United States Supreme Court, set forth his convictions about the relationship of property rights to a just and productive society in this fashion:

> The right of private property is founded in the nature of men and things . . . Exclusive property multiplies the produce of the earth. Who would cultivate the soil and sow the grain if he had no special interest in the harvest? Who would rear and tend the flocks and herds if they could be taken from him by anyone who should come to demand them? . . . What belongs to no one is wasted by everyone. What belongs to one man in particular is the object of his economy and care. Exclusive property prevents disorder and promotes peace.

Well, the purpose of this sampling of colonial commentary is not to imply that these men were faultless paragons of virtue. They were not. They were human and they committed sins and errors. Nevertheless, they were imbued with a strong moral sense and they were earnestly concerned with implementing it in the life of the society. I think it is clear that the reaction of the colonies to the oppression of the British government was not solely the natural resentment stimulated by a tyrant's disregard for the interests and the property of remote colonists; their anger was heightened and multiplied by a burning sense of injustice.

There is, I think, a parallel in the moral impetus which brought the Pilgrims to Plymouth Rock and that which led to the decision for independence 156 years later. Just as the intense desire for the freedom to live by their religious convictions inspired the settlers of New England to undertake the dangerous and arduous task of founding a new home in the wilderness, so the intense desire for the freedom to live according to political and economic justice in-

spired the residents of the thirteen colonies to undertake the dangerous and arduous task of defying the mother country.

The Liberty Bell which the Province of Pennsylvania had ordered for its State House in 1751 had been muffled to ring out the symbolic "death" of liberty in 1765 when the Stamp Act was enforced, and muffled again to mark the closing of Boston Harbor on June 1, 1774. On July 8, 1776, the Liberty Bell called the citizens of Philadelphia to hear a public reading of the Declaration of Independence. King George and his government had grievously violated their own sacred honor through a long series of arbitrary, immoral and unjust acts and the colonists, having earnestly tried to bring about a more reasonable relationship, concluded that "the Laws of Nature and Nature's God" morally entitled them to release from his tyranny.

When the war was finally ended, the work of establishing the new government began. The framers of the United States Constitution and the advocates who wrote analyses in support of its adoption carried on the profound concern for what is right and what is wrong in human conduct. They wished to guard against human weaknesses and, through the separation of powers, sought to ensure responsible liberty against the impulse to gain greater and greater control which throughout history has been irresistible to some leaders. It was hoped to create a government framework which would provide a maximum reenforcement of freedom, but there was also a full recognition that the ultimate and irreducible requirement of freedom is a virtuous and honorable citizenry.

This double concern is repeatedly expressed in George Washington's "Farewell Address to the People of the United States." In speaking to his first major point—the preservation of the Union—he expressed the hope "that your union and brotherly affection may be perpetual—that the free constitution, which is the work of your hands, may be sacredly maintained—that its administration in every de-

partment may be stamped with wisdom and virtue . . . This
government, . . . completely free in its principles, in the
distribution of its powers, uniting security with energy, and
containing within itself provision for its own amendment,
has a just claim to your confidence and support. Respect
for its authority, compliance with its laws, acquiescence in
its measures, are duties enjoined by the fundamental maxims
of true liberty." Later in the speech, he says, "Of all the
dispositions and habits which lead to political prosperity,
religion and morality are indispensable supports." Toward
the conclusion, he comments briefly on his stewardship in
public office. "How far in the discharge of my official duties,
I have been guided by the principles which have been de-
lineated, the public records and other evidences of my
conduct must witness to you and to the world. —To myself,
the assurance of my own conscience is that I have at least
believed myself to be guided by them." Of all the extraordinary men of that period, certainly none had a greater
concern than George Washington for honorable conduct
and no one embodied it so fully in his service.

Before offering some thoughts about the significance of
this concept for us today, I think it may be useful to
identify certain key elements within the colonial conception of honorable conduct which were believed indispensable to the existence of responsible freedom. They are
self-discipline, self-reliance, respect for the law, respect for
private property, all pervaded by an unselfish concern for
the public good.

Times have changed. Morality has been scoffed and
scorned into a small corner. Certainly no responsible observer of this society would judge any of the four—self-
discipline, self-reliance, respect for the law or respect for
private property—to be a dominant characteristic of our
nation today. These traits are on the wane. Well, what
about liberty? How is it faring? I imagine most people
would assert that liberty is still with us and in fairly good
health.

Well, is it? The governmental regulatory mechanisms
have been multiplying at a dizzying rate. There is scarcely
any organized activity left in our society that is not subject
to a growing array of federal regulations and requirements,
spot checks and penalties for noncompliance. In the educational profession, people assumed until quite recently
that academic freedom was an impenetrable bulwark against
outside interference. Well, whether you consider it a civic
triumph or something less than that, affirmative action
cracked the academic freedom wall wide open and a whole
troop of less publicized but domineering regulations have
rushed into the gap. The latest set of federal controls over
institutional policies has been imposed because of loan
funds obtained by the students from private banks, but
insured and subsidized by the government. (This reasoning
might be compared to the government's dictating to the
landlord the temperature at which he must keep his building because some of the tenants receive Social Security
checks.) More educational controls from headquarters are
waiting in the wings. One interesting bill introduced by
Senators Kennedy and Javits would decide in which communities graduating medical students will be permitted to
begin their medical practice, with such decisions justified
on the grounds that the medical schools have been receiving
federal funds. For the government to determine where
people shall live and work is one of the advanced stages
of tyranny.

In the business world, the heavy hand of government is
even more pervasive and more oppressive. In the last
several years, I have attended a number of conventions held
by various industries. With some regularity, the most
pressing agenda item is how that particular industry can
accommodate itself to, or even survive under, the newest
regulatory burdens imposed by our government. We should,
perhaps, remember that the tenth grievance cited in the
Declaration of Independence was, "He (King George) has
erected a multitude of New Offices, and sent hither swarms

of Officers to harass our people, and eat out their substance."
I suspect King George's offenses in this respect were quite
modest compared to those of the government we have today.

Despite the enveloping governmental regimentation of
companies, institutions and private agencies, the individual's personal life and his home are still relatively free from
Washington dictates, and so we have the impression that
liberty is alive and well and living in America in 1975.
However, freedom can also be restricted by means other
than authoritarian government. The freedom of our homes
and our personal lives is now threatened by a force that
is growing even faster than the army of bureaucrats, and
which will undoubtedly be even more difficult to counteract. This second source of outwardly imposed restriction is
crime. The statistics on this problem are ominous. There
was a 17 percent increase in the overall crime rate in our
country in 1974. Robberies have increased by 255 percent
in the past 14 years, forcible rape by 143 percent, and
murder by 106 percent. Indeed there were 50 murders on
school and college campuses last year, but that record won't
stand up. There were already 70 by the time the schools
closed last spring, and there are, alas, still some months to
go before the final tally is in.

How does crime relate to our liberty? Let us consider
that matter. Two years ago when I was in Spain with the
Drug Commission, my wife and I had the pleasure of dining
in Madrid with several of our students on the Junior Year
Abroad. When we left the restaurant, one of the students
said goodbye to us as we were getting into the car. It seems
that she was going to walk to a friend's house in that part
of the city. Concerned for the safety of a young woman
walking alone in mid-city at 10:30 at night, I urged her to
let us give her a ride, but she told us that a person could
go anywhere at any hour in Madrid without the slightest
fear of being robbed or molested. The other students assured us of this fact. We Americans are accustomed to
thinking of Spain as a nation where liberty has been sorely

circumscribed by a powerful dictatorship and indeed it has. However, the freedom to go where one pleases at any hour is far greater for the Spanish that it is for us, and it is certainly one of the fundamental components of liberty.

Consider another dimension of crime's imposition on how we lead our lives. Not long ago, I heard a series of advertisements on the radio for a condominium. Of all the features claimed for its fortunate residents, the one which received the greatest emphasis was the maximum security provided by a staff of round-the-clock uniformed armed guards. That phrase, maximum security, formerly was applied to prisons where extra precautions were taken to keep the criminals *in*. Now, with criminals in such great abundance and such a small proportion of them incarcerated, we must have maximum security to keep the criminals *out*, out of our homes and shops, our schools and even our churches. Maximum security homes as contrasted with maximum security prisons: what a sad and alarming commentary on the state of things!

In our own small college, a growing portion of our budget is being preempted by the costs of crime. Not very long ago, we had one night watchman who came on duty after supper to walk around the campus, mostly to provide a quick alert if there were a fire. Now, we are forced to divert an increasing portion of our hard-pressed revenues to replace that which has been stolen, to pay for our much larger security staff and their equipment, and to repair the damage which criminals are inflicting with increasing frequency upon our buildings, our property and equipment. Our freedom to spend our funds for our educational program is being diminished by the tyranny of crime.

As the United States Attorney General indicated last fall, the crime rate continues to increase and we do not know what to do about it. Several weeks ago the *U.S. News & World Report* presented a special article on the situation in American prisons where it says there are major changes in the concept of how the prisoners should be

treated. There has been a widespread disillusionment with the results of the programs to rehabilitate criminals. "Many prison experts . . . have concluded that the rehabilitation system is 'bankrupt.' It is not really reforming criminals." I don't suppose it has occurred to anyone that it is impossible to *re*habilitate that which was not habilitated in the first place. It is a little late to *begin* to teach an individual the obligations of responsible citizenship after he or she has committed a crime serious enough to result in a long prison term.

We seem to have assumed we could sustain an ordered free society in a moral vacuum. It cannot be done. We find ourselves now engaged in one effort after another to patch up and put back together lives that have been damaged by the undisciplined conduct of the individual himself, or by the undisciplined conduct of his neighbors. Whether we are trying to teach virtue to criminals in prison, or diminish political corruption by requiring public reports of campaign contributions, or pass laws about safe cars and safe drugs and affirmative action, or help divorcees or unwed mothers cope with economic and emotional difficulties, or pass gun control legislation to reduce violent crime—all these and hundreds of other remedial activities are simply efforts to counteract the devastating failure to teach our young people their obligations as responsible citizens, responsible marriage partners, responsible parents, responsible managers and employees.

Our liberty is being whipsawed, in the first place by the adjustments we must make in our own lives as the direct result of irresponsible conduct by individuals, and in the second place by the interference of the enormous governmental bureaucracy created to do two things: to try to force virtue upon certain selfish and destructive citizens, and to assist certain other citizens who have been victimized by the destructive and selfish conduct of their neighbors. Having failed to teach our people self-reliance, self-discipline, respect for private property, respect for the laws

and a genuine commitment to the public good, we are forced to create layer after layer of costly and often wasteful government to try to counteract this failure. It is a vicious circle which can only continue to get worse until the whole nation, like New York City, is unable to pay for it, or until we recognize what has happened and begin the terribly difficult and unpopular chore of climbing out of the moral swamp back to the firm ground of a citizenry broadly committed, by their honor, to living virtuously.

It is not a new trouble we face. Three hundred years ago, it was already a commonplace. In his work *Samson Agonistes,* John Milton wrote:

> But what more oft, in nations grown corrupt
> And by their vices brought to servitude,
> Than to love bondage more than liberty—
> Bondage with ease than strenuous liberty.

Far easier, we suppose, to expect the government to impose such virtue as we have to have than for each citizen to take upon himself the strenuous burden of a virtuous life. It is time to recognize that doing one's own thing is totally incompatible with responsible liberty. This, I believe, is what Solzhenitsyn had in mind when he said. "I insist that the problems of the West are not political. They are psychological and moral."

It may be that our preference as a nation will be to continue down the road we are traveling, hoping for the best. If, however, there should be sufficient desire to try to redevelop the conditions of liberty, where would we turn? How would we go about it? Let me suggest only one first step. We would have to do away with the silly myth that values and attitudes cannot be taught, that virtue, where it occurs, is merely a biological accident. It is a comfortable myth for the teacher who believes it, because the teacher is thus freed to do his own thing unhindered by any gnawing thought that what takes place in the classroom may detract from the dignity of the student's future life

or seriously damage the character of the society in which they both live.

Myth it most certainly is, however. Does anyone really suppose that just by a quirk of fate the millions of people of Soviet Russia hold the views they do and sustain the monstrous system of government described so painfully by Solzhenitsyn? On the other hand, I submit that the wildest coincidence possible among the laws of probability could not account for the fact that all fifty-six signers of the Declaration of Independence inherited by biological accident a sense of honor sufficient to hold them to their pledge under the stresses to which they were later subjected. Patrick Henry, you will recall, stated that the code by which he lived was *instilled* in him by his uncle. In that society the child was instructed from the beginning in what was right and what was virtuous, and the child was encouraged to do right and be virtuous by the joint efforts of family, church and school. The great emphasis was upon obligations and duties in an effort to assist the individual toward full moral maturity.

In higher education today, the reigning philosophy is governed by a value-free concept. How the student, and everyone else, behaves is his own business. Every view of everything is granted equal status and the only offense is to insist that one view is more important than the others. The results of such a philosophy are predictable. Self-discipline lapses if there are no acknowledged evils to avoid. There is no incentive to self-reliance if there is no acknowledged concept of human dignity. If a law is found inconvenient, one simply disregards it, as in the case of using marihuana. Value-free education simply annuls virtue, for virtuous conduct requires a specific understanding of what is right and what is wrong, and behavior consistent with that understanding. Value-free education leaves everyone free to indulge his whims and his passions without regard to the laws or the general welfare. It is a blueprint for

anarchy, and, to some extent, an unintentional training ground for crime.

I think it is useful to try to understand the change in educational philosophy that has taken place over the last two hundred years. The ascendancy of value-free education was not the result of mere perverseness. It has generated great support precisely because it represents the fulfillment of one of the most fundamental principles of liberty—what might be called the political principle. That principle, reenforced by the First Amendment, asserts that every citizen has the right to his own beliefs, to express them publicly and to engage in partisan activities in their behalf. This is, and must continue to be, the right of a free citizen.

There is, however, another principle of liberty, of at least equal importance, that sometimes stands in conflict with the political principle. It is the educational principle. It assumes that man can learn from experience, that knowledge has something to teach ignorance, that informed judgment should prevail over raw judgment. Unfortunately the political principle has to a great extent overwhelmed the educational principle and our society finds itself turmoiled by the moral shambles which has resulted. At our own college where we have faithfully tried to sustain the educational principle, it becomes an interesting challenge as a growing percentage of people arrive here never having heard of the educational principle as it applies to human conduct.

Our nation must, I believe, reassert the educational principle to try to train our people in the requirements of responsible liberty, and do so, not by going to the other extreme and suppressing the political principle, but by seeking out those accommodations which will permit both to operate in their proper spheres. A good example of such an accommodation is offered by Benjamin Franklin's response to certain requests. He refused to print in his newspaper certain slanderous stories brought to him by interested

parties. He volunteered to publish the stories as a separate piece, bearing the author's name and printed at the author's expense, but Franklin set certain standards for his newspaper which he would not compromise.

So I think it should be for a responsible educational institution, and so it was, without question for the educational influences which bore on the lives of the people who brought this nation into being.

Let me conclude with a quotation and an observation. The quotation comes from Andrew Hacker's book, *The End of The American Era*, published in 1968. He asserts:

> Only a few decades remain to complete the era America will have known as a nation. For the United States has embarked on its decline since the closing days of the Second World War . . . It is too late in our history to restore order or reestablish authority: the American temperament has passed the point where self-interest can subordinate itself to citizenship.

*For the student and the faculty member who gives any serious thought to the state of the society and its probable future,* Mr. Hacker has brutally identified the basic question. Has the American temperament reached the point where self-interest cannot subordinate itself to citizenship? Is the individual commitment to public and private virtue irredeemably lost in our society? This is the question faced in microcosm by our college and every other institution. Although Andrew Hacker is widely respected as a scholar and a thinker, I do not share his pessimism. I do not believe the continued disintegration of our society is inevitable, and one of the strongest reasons for my attitude is the study I have done in preparation for this paper. A number of our problems come into focus through contemplating the philosophy and the judgments of the intelligent, courageous, wise and virtuous people who founded this nation in far more difficult circumstances than we face today.

Through the coming year we will have a prolonged opportunity to renew our own courage, develop needed per-

spective, and draw inspiration from studying the most remarkable group of people ever to work together in the western hemisphere for a common worthy purpose, impelled by a sense of "sacred Honor."

# WE HOLD THESE TRUTHS [3]

## WILLIAM E. EVERHEART [4]

William E. Everheart, president of Drury College of Springfield, Missouri, was invited as the featured speaker at Junior Achievement Day at the Kansas City Rotary Club, meeting at noon, January 27, 1976, at the Muehlebach Hotel, Kansas City, Missouri. During the morning the presidents of the junior companies (made up of high school students) had visited the companies of Rotary members, meeting executives and viewing the operations of the various businesses. The students were invited to lunch as guests of the Rotary members. Dr. Everheart's audience numbered approximately eight hundred.

Well aware of the attitudes of students, Everheart met head-on the problem of lethargy by asking his listeners, "Why celebrate then (1876)? Why celebrate now?" In about thirty minutes, he presented "four great commitments" of "the men and women who founded this nation": "the presence and power of God," "the dignity of the individual," "the significance of individual enterprise," and "the commitment with their talents, their money and their lives." He skillfully wove into his presentation numerous quotations from Thomas Jefferson, George Washington, John Hancock, and the Declaration of Independence. In addition, he amplified his theme with apt paraphrases or quotations drawn from Martin Diamond, C. S. Lewis, Abraham Lincoln, James Russel Lowell, Theodore Roosevelt, and Jean Jaurès.

When a speaker uses quotations he may give the appearance of having too little of his own to say. "He just stuck together a lot of quotes," say the students. However, Everheart made each quotation further his message and at the same time maintained coherence. He kept his speech "marching toward its goal." This brief speech demonstrated the characteristics of the classical epideictic speech as described by Aristotle. Like great ceremonial speakers of the past, Everheart in his final paragraphs said that

[3] Delivered at Junior Achievement Day at the Kansas City Rotary Club, at the Muehlebach Hotel, Kansas City, Missouri. January 22, 1976. Quoted by permission.

[4] For biographical note, see Appendix.

we celebrate the occasion "to stimulate our appreciation of the past—the rock on which this republic was built" and second to "stimulate our preparation for and participation in the future." Similar sentiments were expressed by Daniel Webster one hundred and fifty years ago in his speeches known as the Plymouth Oration and the Bunker Hill Monument Orations.

This speech presents an interesting contrast to the one Dr. John Howard delivered at the opening convocation of Rockford College in September 1975. Each in its own way is most appropriate to commemorate the two hundredth anniversary of the signing of the Declaration of Independence.

Our country has begun the Bicentennial celebration. Many of us may wonder in these days of recession, inflation, worldwide unrest, unemployment and pessimism, if we really have anything to celebrate.

Doubtless a great many people had much the same questions in 1876 when we observed our centennial. For example, in that year the memory of the Civil War was still vivid. Even as Philadelphia began its centennial observance, word came that General Custer's command had been slaughtered at the Little Big Horn. Samuel B. Tilden had outpolled Rutherford B. Hayes but Congress handed the presidency to Hayes anyway. The Ku Klux Klan was riding high, and Texas was living under lynch law. President Grant's Administration had been virtually dismantled by scandal. The country was still reeling from the 1873 panic and workers found their incomes slashed by as much as 50 percent during the centennial year.

Why celebrate then? Why celebrate now?

I believe we have genuine reason for celebration and for many reasons. Time will only permit me to mention one of them, but I hope it will help to set in deserved perspective the significance of this Bicentennial event.

Today I want to emphasize the richness and strength of our heritage. We joke a lot about the Founding Fathers. A few days ago I was reading about a young student who was

asked to write an essay on the life of Benjamin Franklin. He squirmed in his chair, chewed his pencil, took a piece of paper, wrote at the top of it, "Benjamin Franklin," and produced the following masterpiece:

Benjamin Franklin was born in Boston, but he soon got tired of that and moved to Philadelphia. When he got to Philadelphia he was hungry so he bought a loaf of bread. He put the bread under his arm. He walked up the street. He passed a woman. The woman smiled at him. He married the woman and discovered electricity.

The men and women who founded this nation were motivated by four great commitments:

*First*, they acknowledged the presence and power of God. In 1774, Thomas Jefferson wrote: "The God who gave us life, gave us liberty at the same time: the hand of force may destroy but cannot disjoin them."

In his first inaugural address, April 30, 1789, George Washington declared:

It would be peculiarly improper to omit in this first official act, my fervent supplications to that almighty being who rules over the universe, who presides in the councils of nations, and whose providential aids can supply every human defect, that his benediction may consecrate to the liberties and happiness of the people of the United States, a government instituted by themselves for these essential purposes: . . . No people can be bound to acknowledge and adore the invisible hand, which conducts the affairs of men, more than the people of the United States. Every step, by which they have advanced to the character of an independent nation, seems to have been distinguished by some token of providential agency.

This is why the Declaration of Independence uses such language as "endowed by their creator," "appealing to the supreme judge of the world," and "with a firm reliance on divine providence."

*Second*, they proclaimed the dignity of the individual. "We," they declared, "hold these truths to be self-evident,

that all men are created equal, that they are endowed by their creator with certain unalienable rights, that among these are life, liberty and the pursuit of happiness." They wanted the world to hear their commitment to equality. People, they declared, are equal—not in mental capacity, physical size, ability or attractiveness—but equally free, equally possessors of certain unalienable rights, equal before the law and in the judgment of God.

They proclaimed equality. They also talked about rights, and the primary right upon which they concentrated was that of liberty—freedom to live and to pursue happiness.

Dr. Martin Diamond, distinguished interpreter of the thoughts of America's founders, put it this way in an address at Independence Square, Philadelphia:

> What was truly revolutionary in the American Revolution and its Declaration of Independence was that liberty, civil liberty —the doctrine of certain unalienable rights—was made the end of government. Not, as had been the case for millennia, whatever end *power* haphazardly imposed upon government; nor any longer the familiar variety of ends—not virtue, not piety, not privilege or wealth, not merely protection, and not empire and dominion; but now deliberately the principle of liberty.

Thomas Jefferson laid the cornerstone in these memorable words: "Freedom of religion, freedom of the press, and freedom of habeas corpus . . . these principles . . . guided our steps through an age of revolution and reformation."

*Third*, they emphasized the significance of individual enterprise. It has been suggested that they never dreamed of any other economic system than the one Adam Smith proposed in the *Wealth of Nations*, which interestingly enough was published in 1776.

Undoubtedly this is why Thomas Jefferson wrote: "Agriculture, manufacture, commerce and navigation, the

four pillars of our prosperity, are the most thriving when left to individual enterprise."

Surely across these two hundred years our forefathers would warn us that when "we the people" become "they the government" the bells of doom have already begun to toll.

*Fourth*, they sealed their commitment with their talents, their money, and their lives. The last line of the declaration reads: "and for the support of this declaration, with a firm reliance on the protection of divine providence, we mutually pledge to each other our lives, our fortunes and our sacred honor." And they meant it!

Early in the American Revolution, a force led by George Washington lay siege to Boston, the headquarters of a British army under Lord Howe. The siege successfully contained the British, but was not forcing them out of Boston.

Washington hesitated to bombard the town for fear of destroying a great deal of property owned by American patriots. Some of the leaders of the Revolution were from Boston. Washington finally consulted the Continental Congress, explaining the advantages of bombardment and why he hesitated.

John Hancock, one of those who later signed the Declaration of Independence, addressed the chair: "It is true, Sir, nearly all the property I have in this world is in houses and other real estate in the town of Boston; but if the liberties of our country require their being burnt to ashes —issue the order for that purpose immediately."

Why is it so important for us to review the record? There are at least two reasons:

*First*, such reflection will, hopefully, stimulate our appreciation of the past—the rock on which this republic

was built. C. S. Lewis, brilliant teacher at Oxford and atheist become Christian, said shortly before his death: "Those who do not know history will be victims of recent bad history."

Abraham Lincoln caught the vision in these most provocative lines:

> . . . Something is in that declaration giving liberty,
> Not alone to the people of this country,
> But hope to the world for all future time.
> It was that which gave promise
> That in due time the weights should be lifted
> From the shoulders of all men,
> And that all should have an equal chance.
> This is the sentiment embodied
> In that Declaration of Independence.

*Second,* such reflection will also, hopefully, stimulate our preparation for and participation in the future. When the French historian Guizot asked James Russell Lowell how long the American Republic would last, Lowell is reported to have said, "It will last as long as the ideals of its founders remain dominant."

We, in 1976, have a peculiar responsibility and opportunity to both define and disseminate the ideas and ideals of this great nation to the end that these United States may fulfill, under God, her destiny. The task is not an easy one. Theodore Roosevelt summed it up this way:

> It is not the critic who counts; nor the man who points out how the strong man stumbled, or where the doer of deeds could have done them better. The credit belongs to the man who is actually in the arena, whose face is marred by dust and sweat and blood; who strives valiantly; who errs and comes short again and again; who knows the great enthusiasms, the great devotions; who spends himself in a worthy cause; who, at the best, knows in the end the triumph of high achievement, and who, at the worst, if he fails, at least fails while daring greatly so that his place will never be with those timid souls who know neither victory or defeat.

God give us courage and wisdom, as the French historian, Jean Jaurès, exhorts us: "To take from the altar of the past the fire, not the ashes"—and move forward to make this a more useful nation and a better world.

# OUR BICENTENNIAL [5]

## BILLY GRAHAM [6]

Billy Graham is considered by many to be the greatest contemporary evangelist, one who "is in the same league with Wesley and Moody" (Carl F. H. Henry, former editor of *Christianity Today*, quoted by Clive Lawrence in *Christian Science Monitor*, February 1, 1974). He has evangelized in Great Britain, France, Germany, Italy, Switzerland, India, the Philippines, Hong Kong, Taiwan, Korea, and Japan. In the late 1950s he attracted over 2 million people to his sixteen-week rally at Madison Square Garden in New York City. In 1960, at the climax of his Los Angeles–Southern California Crusade, he packed into the Los Angeles Memorial Stadium 134,254 persons. In a London crusade in 1966, he spoke to 955,368 persons in a twenty-seven-day meeting (*Current Biography*, January 1973). At his twenty-fifth massive crusade in Korea in 1973, on one occasion he preached to at least 600,000 persons, which "may be the largest audience addressed by a Protestant clergyman." In addition to the more than 60 million that he addressed in person in his three to five major yearly crusades, he is heard weekly by millions more, worldwide, over one thousand radio stations. Clive Lawrence concludes that Billy Graham is "one of the most famous clergymen in the world" (*Christian Science Monitor*, February 1, 1974).

On Wednesday, December 31, 1975, Billy Graham delivered a New Year's Eve Sermon over the ABC, NBC, and Mutual Radio Networks' independent stations and on television over 330 major channels. Appropriately he called his presentation "Our Bicentennial." He opened by relating that he had just returned "from a three-month trip around the world that took me through Asia, various countries in the Middle East and Europe. I have talked with church leaders, political leaders, educators and military leaders. I visited with a number of heads of state." In these sentences, Graham exerted powerful ethos to establish that he was worth listening to.

After quickly establishing that "at home many of our problems are getting worse with every passing day," Graham wove his mes-

[5] Delivered over radio and television, December 31, 1975. Quoted by permission of Billy Graham.

[6] For biographical note, see Appendix.

sage into the warp of the Bicentennial tapestry. Systematically, he developed the contention that "religious influences have helped mold this nation from the beginning," considering chronologically how religious ideals were foremost in the landing of the Pilgrims, the settlement of the Puritans, the Great Awakening, the Declaration of Independence, and in the drafting and ratification of the Constitution. He drew upon these historical examples to give substance to his religious message. Unlike many of Graham's crusade sermons that are filled with citations from Scripture, this exhortation draws upon historical citation for its persuasive power. The speaker sought a much broader audience than he does in his more evangelistic efforts.

Reminiscent of the power of Jonathan Edwards' "Sinners in the Hands of an Angry God" were many intense appeals to fear: "The Atomic Clock [moves] closer to midnight"; "recently . . . highly trained terrorists have arrived in the United States"; "judgment is going to fall upon us in a very short time"; "will America continue on the broad road that leads to destruction"; "America is too young to die." But these motivations drew not upon the Devil, but upon threats to the civil order.

Of course in his solution steps he reasserted his fundamentalist position: "recognize that God loves you," "be honest before God," "receive Jesus Christ," "be a living example by your good works." In his final point, he suggested what could be termed a social gospel: "get involved in the political process . . . We need men and women of integrity and Christian commitment who will run for political office this coming year."

This sermon did not suggest "the fiery Bible thumping, finger-jabbing Graham of 'the sawdust trail' " (*Current Biography*, January 1973), but seemed instead to give the impression of an "ecumenical position of enlightened fundamentalism" (phrase from Edward B. Fiske, religious editor of the New York *Times*). More thoughtful than emotional, it suggested that Graham has a good sense of history. But it also reflected his "enormous religious conviction" (Clive Lawrence).

Graham has mastered the modern mass media, whether in the spotlight before thousands, before a microphone in a studio, or caught by a television camera. In person or over radio and television, he is a powerful speaker with a "striking appearance, Shakespearean gestures, a flexible voice and perfectly timed dramatic pauses." Clive Lawrence observes:

> When Billy Graham steps to the podium in New York, Hong Kong, London, or Seoul, people listen. He is over 6

feet. His face is sculptured, as if out of fine wood; his eyes are deepset and burn with conviction.

He speaks in a rich, modified Southern accent, and frequently pauses while his words cut into consciousness. He extols with a fine hand pointing skyward. He confides with his palm on the Bible. He challenges with a knotted fist. He invites with open arms. (*Christian Science Monitor,* February 1, 1974)

Good evening!

I have just returned from a three-month trip around the world that took me through Asia, various countries in the Middle East and Europe. I have talked with church leaders, political leaders, educators, and military leaders. I visited with a number of heads of state. I wish that every American could have been with me on this trip. It has been an eye opener! For example, someone has said that if you haven't been in Asia in the last six months you don't know Asia. The world is changing so rapidly that I hardly know it any more.

At midnight we enter 1976, the year of our two hundredth birthday, with a paradox of moods on the part of the American people. On the one hand, many are excited, thrilled, and optimistic about the next year. On the other hand, as a news magazine says, "Americans are in a bitter and fearful mood." There is no doubt that many are confused, discouraged, cynical, afraid, and disillusioned—with our scientists warning us of an all-out atomic war before the end of the century.

While we Americans will be glued to our television screens tomorrow watching the football games, the rest of the world is reeling and rocking from crisis to crisis. Dangerous explosions are almost everywhere. We are on the edge of a precipice. One newspaper reports that over twenty-five wars have been fought this past year or are now being fought. Most of them do not make the headlines, but people are being wounded and killed. When I hear so much talk of peace, I am reminded of what God said through Jeremiah to the false prophets of his day. God said they

were "shouting peace, peace, when there is no peace." The Psalmist warned about dealing with those whose words are smoother than butter—those who say, "I am for peace," but . . . are for war. Let's face it. There has never been so much talk of peace, nor such a preparation for war as there is today.

Here at home many of our problems are getting worse with every passing day. The crime rate jumped faster than any other year in history. Drug addiction continues to soar as stronger drugs arrive daily by the planeload. Massive debts threaten some of our major cities with bankruptcy. Family life falters, and thousands of children are made orphans every month from broken homes. Abortion has brought the population growth to a standstill.

As I return home, I have a feeling that the American people are almost drugged and are oblivious to the events at home and abroad that cause the Atomic Clock to move closer to midnight.

What is wrong? It is almost a paradox that America, possessing all the economic affluence for enjoying life, virtually leads the world in crime, narcotics abuse, pornography, immorality, and even debts. We seem to be naive to what is happening in the real world. So we watch spectator and entertainment events on television and try to forget it all, hoping that it will go away. Or we take another highball and try to relax.

The rest of the world watches our self-inflicted wounds with amazement. They cannot understand why we wash so much dirty linen in public.

Tonight, before we take a look at the future, we should look at the past and remind ourselves of the roots from which we sprang two hundred years ago.

I do not see how anyone could study the history of America without recognizing religious influences that have helped mold this nation from the beginning.

In 1835, an astute French visitor to the United States reported, "Upon my arrival in the United States, the re-

ligious aspect of the country was the first thing that struck my attention."

In no other nation's founding documents can we find so many declarations of allegiance to God. Time after time in our history there have been appeals to the "Supreme Judge" in seeking to build a new nation. This idea of freedom as a "right" of all men everywhere is absolutely unique among nations.

But where did it come from? Any search for its origin takes us back to "our fathers' God . . . Author of liberty." It takes us to the creation of man, whom God made in His own likeness, free to roam and replenish the earth. Free to decide *how* or even *whether* he would serve his Creator. And man chose rebellion. Today because of that choice by our first parents, we are alienated from God. Because of this alienation we are a "suffering" planet, with the ultimate result of "death" for every generation.

But this idea of freedom also takes us back to the Old Testament prophets, proclaiming in the face of kings and shouting from dungeons man's God-endowed right to freedom under God.

It takes us back to an angry Moses, daring Pharaoh's wrath to demand, "Let my people go!" and later leading a great army of the enslaved into a new country where they could, at God's behest, "proclaim liberty throughout the land and to all the inhabitants thereof." These words from Leviticus 25:10 are inscribed on America's Liberty Bell in Philadelphia.

It takes us back to Jesus Christ who, standing in Nazareth, boldly declared His destiny—"to preach deliverance to the captives, to set at liberty them that are bruised."

Liberty and freedom—these were the flaming revolutionary words the early followers of Christ cast again and again into the tinderbox of men's hearts and hopes.

Now, the thing tyrants feared was this ideal of the Free Man in God. That ideal has always been terrifying to tyrants and that is why religious liberty is being curtailed

in so many parts of the world today. Give men the Bible and freedom to proclaim its message, and they will soon be free.

It was in pursuit of this ideal that those 102 brave men and women clambered aboard a tiny vessel called the Mayflower one chill day in 1620 and, with prayers on their lips and visions of a new "nation under God," set sail for a far, unknown land.

The night before that historic dawn when the Pilgrims landed, they had crowded into her tiny hold to sign their "Mayflower Compact" (based on Biblical principles as they saw them)—later to be called "the birth certificate of American democracy."

And the Puritans who followed during the great migrations of 1630-1640 also "laid it on the line"—their reasons for coming to Massachusetts Bay. The opening sentence of their "New England Confederation" says, "We all came into these parts of America with one and the same end, namely, to advance the Kingdom of the Lord Jesus Christ." Not all, of course, were dedicated Christians. After the Puritans, there came a diverse lot of adventurers, slave traders, ex-prisoners and unbelievers. But it is a mark of the Puritans' vitality that their ideals largely prevailed in early America.

Americans who scoff at their straight-lacedness and earlier intolerance should never forget that it was the Puritan's religious faith and his passion for self-rule that gave us much of our system of political and social democracy—that has lasted these two hundred years.

But both patriotism and Puritanism tended to wane and weaken in the third generation. By the middle of the eighteenth century, problems for the young country began to mount. Many of them are the problems we face today. For example, inflation is nothing new in American history. In the late 1700s, during the days of the American Revolution, they too faced inflation. In 1779, ducks and chickens were sold for a few pennies each. In just two years' time they were costing $250 each. There came a time that money was

hardly worth the paper it was printed on. That money, issued by the Continental Congress, had become valueless.

We should remember, as we face inflation today, that it's not nearly so bad as was faced by our forebears, and they licked it by sheer courage, discipline, hard work, and faith in the future of America.

Remember, the people that founded America did not have telephones, radio, television, electricity, automobiles, airplanes, inside plumbing, or refrigerators. They had no tractors or bulldozers. They had no supermarkets. They had no Social Security or guaranteed welfare. The fastest they could travel was by horseback. Yet they succeeded—where we seem to be failing. They scratched, dug, worked, sweated, and prayed to build a nation from New York to San Francisco.

Many times during American history there have been great spiritual awakenings that have affected the nation and strengthened its moral and spiritual fabric. One of those was called "The Great Awakening" of the 1740s. It strengthened the nation for the bitter days of the Revolution. Great evangelists like George Whitefield and Jonathan Edwards proclaimed judgment and grace, calling on the people to turn to God.

This Great Awakening, say historians, cradled and paved the way for the Revolution. Under such eloquent preaching sat those young people who would soon be called "the Founding Fathers" of America. And from under such preaching came men like John Adams who wrote, "Statesmen may plan and speculate for liberty, but it is religion and morality alone upon which freedom can securely stand. A patriot must be a religious man."

The Declaration of Independence reflects the feelings of men to whom religious faith was all-important. There was not an atheist or an agnostic among the fifty-six who signed that Declaration, though some were deists. Before they strode forward to append their signatures, each bowed his head in prayer. The Declaration's giant step was being

taken, they affirmed, "with a firm reliance upon the protection of Divine Providence." In declaring themselves free, they said, they were assuming "the separate and equal station to which the laws of God entitled them." The self-evident truth they voiced was that men were "endowed by their Creator" with inalienable rights. And before the world they appealed to "the Supreme Judge of the world" for the source of their intentions.

Such expressions were no mere polite gestures to God. They were a firm commitment to the principle that God must be central to any plan of government. Because they signed that document, some of those men were captured and hanged. Some were stripped of their possessions, some were jailed. I have to ask myself tonight, at another hour of American crisis, do we have that kind of courage? Would we be willing to sign? How many people today would be willing to put their life on the line for freedom?

Eleven years later, *after* the Revolution was won, there assembled in Philadelphia men from thirteen colonies charged with creating one of the most revolutionary political documents of all time.

Yet there were flaws. They were men who had never known the concept of democratic liberty and freedom. For example, slavery was a part of the social structure, both North and South. Catholics could vote in only three of the thirteen states. Jews were not permitted to vote in New Jersey or in New Hampshire. Women could not vote anywhere in America. In the hindsight of two hundred years, they made many mistakes, but what they produced was nothing short of a miracle of God.

When the Constitution was submitted for ratification, the people demanded a Bill of Rights that would settle certain fundamental freedoms once and for all. They were implied in the Constitution, but the people wanted them in black and white. In the Amendments making up the Bill of Rights, where was religion? *First!* In top place! Speech, Assembly and Petition followed Religion in the

First Amendment. These were quickly approved. But for three and a half months the House and Senate debated the phrasing of Religious Freedom, changing the words around, adding, deleting, clarifying. At no time in history has so much care and attention been lavished on one sentence of legislation.

The final wording: "Congress shall make no law respecting an establishment of religion, or prohibiting the free exercise thereof." It was not government renouncing religious faith; it was government protecting our religious faith by forever removing "religious rights" from tampering by any public authority or self-seeking hierarchy. Here we have a guarantee that America would never have a civil religion. But we would have freedom of religion—not freedom from religion as some have mistakenly interpreted this Amendment.

In every area of American life, the "faith of our fathers" has left its indelible imprint. And nowhere more so than in its educational system. When our forefathers stepped ashore in the New World, their first act was to establish a home. Next, they erected a church. Then they started a school.

The Puritans and the Pilgrims came to the New World determined to provide education for their young. In the lands they'd left, education was the privilege of the few. Therefore, those early Americans flung up their rude schoolhouses all along the advancing frontier. Their first textbook was the Bible, their first task to teach children to read.

Founded also by the churches were America's first institutions of higher learning. A few years after the Pilgrims landed, Harvard College came into being—its motto: "For Christ and the Church"; its main purpose: a training center for clergy. In 1701, Yale College was founded by a group of evangelical clergymen for the same purpose. Princeton was brought into being by the Presbyterian "revivalist party." The University of Pennsylvania stemmed

directly from George Whitefield's electrifying preaching during the Great Awakening.

It was in America's churches too that women first came into their own. The Pilgrim woman was a new breed. Along with her man she stepped onto those free shores with freedom shining in her eyes. At home, in her community and church, she began her God-given fulfillment as a woman.

We may be a vastly different people today than we were two hundred years ago. Our society is far more complex, more pluralistic. But of this we can be sure—God has not changed. His laws have not changed. He is still a God of love and mercy—but He is also a God of righteousness and judgment. Any individual or nation which ignores His moral and spiritual laws will ultimately face His judgment.

I believe that every problem facing us tonight as Americans is basically a spiritual problem. Crime is a spiritual problem. Inflation is a spiritual problem. Corruption is a spiritual problem. Social injustice is a spiritual problem. The lack of a "will" even to defend our freedoms is a spiritual problem.

The Lord, speaking through His servant, the prophet Isaiah, said,

I was ready to be sought by those who did not ask for me. I was ready to be found by those who did not seek me. I said, Here am I, to a nation that did not call on my name. I spread out my hands all the day to a rebellious people who follow their own devices. A people who provoke me to my face continually. . . . When I spoke, you did not listen, but you did that which was evil in my eyes.

And judgment came!

The great question before us tonight, on the eve of our two hundredth birthday and on the eve of 1976—a crucial election year—is: will this nation survive this century as a free society, or even the next five years as a free society? As I came home from my three-month world tour, this is

how crucial and how critical the problems of the present hour seem to me. I do not believe that we will be a free democracy twenty-four years from now in the year 2000, unless a dramatic change takes place within the hearts of the people of this nation.

It was James Russell Lowell, American poet of the last century, who put the challenge to us. When asked by a French historian, "How long do you think the American republic will endure?" Lowell replied, "So long as the ideas of its Founding Fathers continue to be dominant!"

One of the ideas was that the Bible was true, and that our entire social and political structure was to be built upon its laws and teachings.

Another idea that our Founding Fathers had was that God was supreme. That is why they put on our coins, "In God We Trust."

Another early idea, not shared by all by any means, was that every person needed Jesus Christ in his heart.

As tonight we enter a historic year, America is troubled. Our people are filled with frustration, fear, and confusion. According to a series of articles in the Los Angeles *Times* in October [1975], thousands of radicals are highly organized from coast to coast with the determination to overthrow this country. We have heard testimony before Congress recently that highly trained terrorists have arrived in the United States to begin terror tactics during the Bicentennial year.

Will they succeed? It will depend on the patriotism, courage and faith such as those early Americans had, when they landed on these shores. Is God going to allow a cataclysmic judgment to fall upon this nation as has fallen upon nations of the past who have turned from God and forgotten Him? Or will God send to us another great spiritual awakening that has saved us in the past?

During the last twelve months, thousands of Americans have been turning to God. Prayer groups and Bible study groups have been springing up all over the nation. Churches

and other religious organizations are reporting that millions
are living a more disciplined Christian life. This is encouraging—even though it only involves a minority.

In a time similar to ours, when only a minority were
true believers, Isaiah the great Hebrew prophet said, "Except the Lord of hosts had left unto us a very small rem-
nant, we should have been like Sodom, and we should have
been like unto Gomorrah."

But God is warning us tonight that judgment is going
to fall upon us in a very short time unless we as a nation
repent and turn to God. In pleading with ancient Israel,
God said,

Come now, and let us reason together, saith the Lord: though
your sins be as scarlet, they shall be as white as snow; though they
be red like crimson, they shall be as wool. If ye be willing and
obedient, ye shall eat the good of the land. *But* if ye refuse and
rebel, ye shall be devoured with the sword; for the mouth of the
Lord hath spoken it.

Will America turn to God at this late hour, or will
America continue on the broad road that leads to destruction? It will soon be too late to decide—already the storm
clouds are gathering.

I am calling Christians everywhere to a time of humilia-
tion, prayer, and fasting during this two hundredth anniversary. There is no possible solution to the problems we
face apart from a change in the spiritual atmosphere.

You who are listening to me tonight are asking the question, "What can I as an individual do? I feel so helpless in
the midst of the present crisis. I want to do something—
but what?"

What did those early pastors, teachers and evangelists
proclaim? The heart of the message of Whitefield, Edwards,
Wesley, Tennent and hundreds of other clergy along the
frontier was basically the same message I offer to you tonight.

*First,* recognize that God loves you. The Bible says that

He is not willing that any should perish but that all should come to repentance.

*Second,* be honest before God. Admit that you have broken His laws and chosen to go your own way instead of His way. Be willing to let Him change your life.

*Third,* receive Jesus Christ into your heart as Savior and Lord.

*Fourth,* be a living example by your good works. The apostle James said, "Faith without works is dead." This proves that you mean business with God. Pray for those in authority—be a good citizen—help the poor—help the distressed and help the oppressed of the world.

*Fifth,* get involved in the political process. This coming year is an election year. I would like to challenge every deeply committed American who is qualified to think about running for political office. I do not believe that we as Christians should withdraw. We need men and women of integrity and Christian commitment who will run for political office this coming year—no matter to which political party you belong. On this New Year's Eve, if you will do these things you could have a part in helping America be the kind of country you want for your children and grandchildren.

America is too young to die. She is only two hundred years old. During the last few weeks I have been in countries that date their history back thousands of years. We are a young country and should be just getting started. But unless we wake up and accept the challenge handed to us by our forefathers, we will die, like countries and civilizations of the past.

During this past year [1975] Alexander Solzhenitsyn visited the United States. While he was here, he told a little story that bears repeating tonight. He said that only once during his long imprisonment in a Soviet Union labor camp did he become so discouraged that he contemplated suicide. He was outdoors on a work detail, and he had reached the point where he didn't care whether the guards

killed him or not. When he had a break, he sat down, and a perfect stranger sat down beside him—someone he had never seen before and never saw again. This stranger took a stick and drew a cross on the ground for no explainable reason. Solzhenitsyn sat and stared at that cross and then said, "I realize therein lies man's freedom." At that point, a new courage and a will to live and work returned.

Tonight you can come to that same cross and find forgiveness, peace, joy, and eternal life. Life takes on a new meaning, a new hope, a new song. This could be your commitment tonight.

May God help you to make this commitment, and may 1976 be a joyous and blessed year for each of you.

# AMERICANS VIEW THEIR
# FOREIGN POLICY

## AMERICA'S PERMANENT INTERESTS [1]

### HENRY A. KISSINGER [2]

In no uncertain terms Henry A. Kissinger, Secretary of State, laid down the following challenge to politicians who were making US foreign policy a 1976 campaign issue:

> Certainly there is room for differences on the policies to be pursued in a complex and dangerous world. But those who challenge current policies have an obligation to go beyond criticisms, slogans, and abuse and set forth in detail their premises and alternatives, the likely costs, opportunities, and risks. . . . The time has come, as Adlai Stevenson said, to ". . . talk sense to the American people." As a nation we face new dangers and opportunities; neither will wait for our decisions next November and both can be profoundly affected by what we say and do in the meantime. Complex realities cannot be dissolved or evaded by nostalgic simplicities.

On March 11, 1976, at a luncheon at the Statler Hilton Hotel, Boston, the Boston World Affairs Council bestowed upon the Secretary of State the Christian A. Herter Award for "contributions to better international understanding." The presentation was made by Henry Cabot Lodge, former American ambassador. In response, Kissinger delivered an address entitled "America's Permanent Interests" to an audience of 850 (Boston *Globe,* March 12, 1976).

To clarify his reason for speaking at Boston on March 11, Henry Kissinger explained: "When over a period of weeks a series of extreme charges are made, actually in both parties, then I feel I have an obligation to put before the public what the foreign policy of this government is and to explain its rationale" (New York *Times,* March 13, 1976). The "extreme charges" had come mainly from Henry Jackson, Democratic senator from Washing-

---

[1] Delivered at a luncheon of the Boston World Affairs Council, Statler Hilton Hotel, Boston, March 11, 1976.
[2] For biographical note, see Appendix.

ton, and Ronald Reagan, Republican opponent of President Ford. They had made Kissinger and his foreign policy a campaign issue. In reply Kissinger gave what *Newsweek* thought was "an unusually acerbic speech" (March 22, 1976). The Boston *Globe* declared the speech more "broad" and "blunt" than any that he presented in the past year.

The speech, a good summary of the foreign policy of the Ford Administration, represented a strong defense of complex negotiations that Kissinger had carried on around the world. It constituted an effective answer to the critics in both parties and in particular Ronald Reagan, who have become increasingly vocal in comments about Angola, the Panama Canal, and relations with the USSR and Cuba. In contrasting Reagan and Kissinger, James M. Perry saw "a classic division": "Reagan's old-fashioned, simplistic . . . approach to world affairs and Kissinger's complex, devious pragmatism" (*National Observer*, February 28, 1976).

The Secretary of State is more likely to win his point by the persuasiveness of his sincerity than by his oratorical prowess. One writer observed, "His heavily accented, metronomic speech delivery does not exactly electrify audiences and . . . his biting wit goes over better in intellectual drawing rooms than among Rotarians." During the past year Kissinger has taken the issues of foreign policy directly to the people (see Leslie H. Gelb, New York *Times*, January 1, 1975). He has addressed audiences in many cities. In reviewing these activities, Kissinger explained: "In the past 14 months alone, I have given 17 major speeches, some 20 major news conferences, and countless interviews across this country, and I have testified 39 times before congressional committees."

I deeply appreciate the honor you bestow upon me today not only because it is given me by old Massachusetts friends, but also for the name it bears. Throughout his long career as legislator, governor, and secretary of state, Christian Herter embodied the ideals of selfless public service and responsible patriotism which have always marked our nation's great leaders. Most of all Christian Herter was a man who had faith in his country and its goodness. He understood the decisive role this nation must play in the world for security and progress and justice.

In this election year, some ten years after Chris Herter's death, we would all do well to remember his wisdom. For America is still the great and good country he knew it was,

and our participation in the international scene remains decisive if our era is to know peace and a better life for mankind. We must never forget that this nation has permanent interests and concerns that must be preserved through and beyond this election year.

This can be a time of national renewal—when Americans freely renegotiate their social compact. Or if the quest for short-term political gain prevails over all other considerations, it can be a period of misleading oversimplification, further divisiveness, and sterile recrimination.

This Administration has for many months been prepared to put its policies, its premises, and its design for the future before the American people. The President has often spoken about our concerns and hopes in the world. In the past 14 months alone, I have given 17 major speeches, some 20 major news conferences, and countless interviews across this country, and I have testified 39 times before congressional committees. Certainly there is room for differences on the policies to be pursued in a complex and dangerous world. But those who challenge current policies have an obligation to go beyond criticisms, slogans, and abuse and set forth in detail their premises and alternatives, the likely costs, opportunities, and risks.

America has come through a difficult time—when our institutions have been under challenge, our purposes doubted, and our will questioned. The time has come, as Adlai Stevenson said, to ". . . talk sense to the American people." As a nation we face new dangers and opportunities; neither will wait for our decisions next November and both can be profoundly affected by what we say and do in the meantime. Complex realities cannot be dissolved or evaded by nostalgic simplicities.

Throughout the turmoil of this decade our foreign policy has pursued our fundamental national goals with energy and consistent purpose.

We are at peace for the first time in over a decade. No American fighting men are engaged in combat anywhere in the world.

Relations with our friends and allies in the Atlantic community and with Japan have never been stronger.

A new and durable relationship with the People's Republic of China has been opened and fostered.

Confrontation in the heart of Europe has been eased. A four-power agreement on Berlin has replaced a decade and a half of crisis and confrontation.

We negotiated an interim agreement limiting strategic arms with the Soviet Union, which forestalled the numerical expansion of Soviet strategic programs while permitting us to undertake needed programs of our own.

We are now negotiating a long-term agreement which, if successfully concluded, will—for the first time in history —set an upper limit on total numbers of strategic weapons, requiring the Soviet Union to dismantle some of its existing systems.

Significant progress toward a durable settlement in the Middle East has been made. Much work and many dangers remain, but the peace process is underway for the first time since the creation of the State of Israel.

There is a new maturity and impetus to our relations with Latin America reflecting changing realities in the hemisphere and the growing importance of these countries on the international scene.

The United States has taken the role of global leadership in putting forward a comprehensive agenda for a new and mutually beneficial relationship between the developed and developing nations.

We have defended human rights and dignity in all international bodies as well as in our bilateral relations.

This is a record of American accomplishment that transcends partisanship, for much of it was accomplished with the cooperation of both parties. It reflects the ideals of the

American people. It portends for this nation a continuing role of moral and political leadership—if we have the understanding, the will, and the unity to seize the opportunity history has given us.

Thirty years ago this country began its first sustained peacetime involvement in foreign affairs. We achieved great things, and we can continue to do so as long as we are prepared to face the fact that we live in a more complex time.

Today the Soviet Union is a superpower. Nothing we could have done would have halted this evolution after the impetus that two generations of industrial and technological advance have given to Soviet military and economic growth. But together with others we must assure that Russian power and influence are not translated into an expansion of Soviet control and dominance beyond the USSR's borders. This is prerequisite to a more constructive relationship.

Today scores of new nations have come into being, creating new centers of influence. These nations make insistent claims on the global system, testing their new economic power and seeking a greater role and share in the world's prosperity.

Today the forces of democracy are called upon to show renewed creativity and vision. In a world of complexity—in a world of equilibrium and coexistence, of competition and interdependence—it is our democratic values that give meaning to our sacrifice and purpose to our exertions. Thus the cohesion of the industrial democracies has a moral as well as a political and economic significance.

Americans are a realistic people who have never considered the definition of a challenge as a prophecy of doom or a sign of pessimism. Instead we have seen it as a call to battle. ". . . the bravest," said Thucydides, "are surely those who have the clearest vision of what is before them, glory and danger alike, and yet notwithstanding go out to

meet it." That has always been the test of democracy—and it has always been the strength of the American people.

Let me now deal with America's permanent interests: peace, progress, and justice.

Since the dawn of the nuclear age, the world's fears of catastrophe and its hopes for peace have hinged on the relationship between the United States and the Soviet Union.

In an era when two nations have the power to visit utter devastation on the world in a matter of hours, there can be no greater imperative than assuring that the relationship between the superpowers be managed effectively and rationally.

This is an unprecedented task. Historically a conflict of ideology and geopolitical interests, such as that which characterizes the current international scene, has almost invariably led to conflict. But in the age of thermonuclear weapons and strategic equality, humanity could not survive such a repetition of history. No amount of tough rhetoric can change these realities. The future of our nation and of mankind depends on how well we avoid confrontation without giving up vital interests and how well we establish a more hopeful and stable relationship without surrender of principle.

We, therefore, face the necessity of a dual policy: On the one hand we are determined to prevent Soviet military power from being used for political expansion; we will firmly discourage and resist adventurist policies. But at the same time we cannot escalate every political dispute into a central crisis; nor can we rest on identifying foreign policy with crisis management. We have an obligation to work for a more positive future. We must couple opposition to pressure and irresponsibility with concerned efforts to build a more cooperative world.

History can inform—or mislead—us in this quest.

For a generation after World War II statesmen and nations were traumatized by the experience of Munich; they

believed that history had shown the folly of permitting an adversary to gain a preponderance of power. This was and remains a crucial lesson.

A later generation was chastened by the experience of Vietnam; it is determined that America shall never again overextend and exhaust itself by direct involvement in remote wars with no clear strategic significance. This too is a crucial lesson.

But equally important and too often neglected is the lesson learned by an earlier generation. Before the outbreak of the first World War, there was a virtual equilibrium of power. Through crisis after crisis nations moved to confrontation and then retreated to compromise. Stability was taken for granted until—without any conscious decision to overturn the international structure—a crisis much like any other went out of control. Nation after nation slid into a war whose causes they did not understand but from which they could not extricate themselves. The result was the death of tens of milllions, the destruction of the global order, and domestic upheavals whose consequences still torment mankind.

If we are to learn from history, we cannot pick and choose the lessons from which we will draw inspiration. The history of this century tells us that:

☐ An imbalance of power encourages aggression;
☐ Overcommitment cannot be sustained domestically; and
☐ An equilibrium based on constant confrontation will ultimately end in cataclysm.

But the lessons of history are never automatic; each generation must apply them to concrete circumstances.

There is no question that peace rests, in the first instance, on the maintenance of a balance of global stability. Without the ultimate sanction of power, conciliation soon

becomes surrender. Moderation is a virtue only in those who are thought to have a choice.

No service is done to the nation by those who portray an exaggerated specter of Soviet power and of American weakness, by those who hesitate to resist when we are challenged, or by those who fail to see the opportunities we have to shape the US-Soviet relationship by our own confident action. Soviet strength is uneven; the weaknesses and frustrations of the Soviet system are glaring and have been clearly documented. Despite the inevitable increase in its power, the Soviet Union remains far behind us and our allies in any overall assessment of military, economic, and technological strength; it would be reckless in the extreme for the Soviet Union to challenge the industrial democracies. And Soviet society is no longer insulated from the influences and attractions of the outside world or impervious to the need for external contacts.

The great industrial democracies possess the means to counter Soviet expansion and to moderate Soviet behavior. We must not abdicate this responsibility by weakening ourselves either by failing to support our defenses or refusing to use our power in defense of our interest; we must, along with our allies, always do what is necessary to maintain our security.

It is true that we cannot be the world's policeman. Not all local wars and regional conflicts affect global stability or America's national interest. But if one superpower systematically exploits these conflicts for its own advantage—and tips the scales decisively by its intervention—gradually the overall balance will be affected. If adventurism is allowed to succeed in local crises, an ominous precedent of wider consequence is set. Other nations will adjust their policies to their perception of the dominant trend. Our ability to control future crises will diminish. And if this pattern is not broken, America will ultimately face harder choices, higher costs, and more severe crises.

But our obligation goes beyond the balance of power. An equilibrium is too precarious a foundation for our long-term future. There is no tranquillity in a balance of terror constantly contested. We must avoid the twin temptations of provocation and escapism. Our course must be steady and not reflect momentary fashions; it must be a policy that our adversaries respect, our allies support, and our people believe in and sustain.

Therefore we have sought with the Soviet Union to push back the shadow of nuclear catastrophe—by settling concrete problems, such as Berlin, so as to ease confrontations and negotiating on limitation of strategic arms to slow the arms race. And we have held out the prospect of cooperative relations in the economic and other fields if political conditions permit their implementation and further development.

It goes without saying that this process requires reciprocity. It cannot survive a constant attempt to seek unilateral advantage. It cannot, specifically, survive any more Angolas. If the Soviet Union is ready to face genuine coexistence, we are prepared to make every effort to shape a pattern of restraint and mutual interest which will give coexistence a more reliable and positive character making both sides conscious of what would be lost by confrontation and what can be gained by cooperation. And we are convinced that when a vigorous response to Soviet encroachment is called for, the President will have the support of the American people—and of our allies—to the extent that he can demonstrate that the crisis was imposed upon us; that it did not result from opportunities we missed to improve the prospects of peace.

No policy will soon, if ever, eliminate the competition and irreconcilable ideological differences between the United States and the Soviet Union. Nor will it make all interests compatible. We are engaged in a protracted process with inevitable ups and downs. But there is no alternative to the policy of penalties for adventurism and incen-

tives for restraint. What do those who speak so glibly about one-way streets or preemptive concessions propose concretely that this country do? What precisely has been given up? What level of confrontation do they seek? What threats would they make? What risks would they run? What precise changes in our defense posture, what level of expenditure over what period of time, do they advocate? How concretely do they suggest managing the US-Soviet relationship in an era of strategic equality?

It is time we heard answers to these questions.

In short we must—and we shall—pursue the two strands of our policy toward the Soviet Union: firmness in the face of pressure and the vision to work for a better future. This is well within our capacities. We owe this to our people, to our future, to our allies, and to the rest of mankind.

The upheavals of this century have produced another task—the fundamental need of reshaping the structure of international relations. For the first time in history the international system has become truly global. Decolonization and the expansion of the world economy have given birth to scores of new nations and new centers of power and initiative. Our current world, numbering nearly 150 nations, can be the seedbed for growing economic warfare, political instability, and ideological confrontation—or it can become a community marked by unprecedented international collaboration. The interdependence of nations—the indivisibility of our security and our prosperity—can accelerate our common progress or our common decline.

Therefore just as we must seek to move beyond a balance of power in East-West relations so must we transcend tests of strength in North-South relations and build a true world community.

We do so in our own self-interest for today's web of economic relationships links the destinies of all mankind. The price and supply of energy, the conditions of trade, the expansion of world food production, the technological bases for economic development, the protection of the

world's environment, the rules of law that govern the world's oceans and outer space—these are concerns that affect all nations and that can be satisfactorily addressed only in a framework of international cooperation.

Here too we need to sustain a complex policy. We must resist tactics of confrontation; but our larger goal must be to shape new international relationships that will last over decades to come. We will not be stampeded by pressures or threats. But it is in our own interest to create an international economic system that all nations will regard as legitimate because they have a stake in it and because they consider it just.

As the world's strongest power, the United States could survive an era of economic warfare. But even we would be hurt, and no American true to the humane heritage of his country could find satisfaction in the world that confrontation would bring in its wake. The benefits of common effort are so apparent and the prospects of economic strife so damaging that there is no moral or practical alternative to a world of expanded collaboration.

Therefore at the World Food Conference in 1974, at the special session of the United Nations General Assembly last September, and in the Conference on International Economic Cooperation now underway in Paris the United States has taken the lead in offering programs of practical cooperation. We have presented—and are vigorously following through—on a wide range of proposals to safeguard export earnings, accelerate industrial and agricultural growth, better conditions of trade and investment in key commodities, and meet the plight of the poorest countries. In every area of concern we have proposed forms of collaboration among *all* nations, including the other industrial countries, the newly wealthy oil producers, and the developing countries themselves.

It is the West—and overwhelmingly this nation—that has the resources, the technology, the skills, the organizational ability, and the goodwill that attract and invite the

cooperation of the developing nations. In the global dialogue among the industrial and developing worlds the Communist nations are conspicuous by their absence and, indeed, by their irrelevance.

Yet at the very moment when the industrial democracies are responding to the aspirations of the developing countries, many of the same countries attempt to extort what has, in fact, been freely offered. Lopsided voting, unworkable resolutions, and arbitrary procedures too often dominate the United Nations and other international bodies. Nations which originally chose nonalignment to shield themselves from the pressures of global coalitions have themselves formed a rigid, ideological, confrontationist coalition of their own. One of the most evident blocs in the world today is, ironically, the almost automatic alignment of the nonaligned.

The United States remains ready to respond responsibly and positively to countries which seriously seek justice and an equitable world economic system. But progress depends on a spirit of mutual respect, realism, and practical cooperation. Let there be no mistake about it: Extortion will not work and will not be supinely accepted. The stakes are too high for self-righteous rhetoric or adolescent posturing.

At issue is not simply the economic arrangements of the next quarter century but the legitimacy of the international order.

Technology and the realities of interdependence have given our generation the opportunity to determine the relationships between the developed and developing countries over the next quarter century. It is the quality of statesmanship to recognize that our necessity, our practical aspirations, and our moral purpose are linked. The United States is ready for that challenge.

Our efforts to build peace and progress reflect our deep-seated belief in freedom and in the hope of a better future for all mankind. These are values we share with our closest allies, the great industrial democracies.

The resilience of our countries in recovering from economic difficulty and in consolidating our cooperation has an importance far beyond our immediate well-being. For while foreign policy is unthinkable without an element of pragmatism, pragmatism without underlying moral purpose is like a rudderless ship.

Together the United States and our allies have maintained the global peace and sustained the world economy for more than thirty years. The spirit of innovation and progress in our societies has no match anywhere, certainly not in societies laying claim to being "revolutionary." Rarely in history have alliances survived—let alone flourished—as ours have in vastly changing global and geopolitical conditions. The ideals of the industrial democracies give purpose to our efforts to improve relations with the East, to the dialogue with the Third World, and to many other spheres of common endeavor.

Our ties with the great industrial democracies are, therefore, not alliances of convenience but a union of principle in defense of values and a way of life.

It is in this context that we must be concerned about the possibility of Communist parties coming to power—or sharing in power—in governments in NATO [North Atlantic Treaty Organization] countries. Ultimately the decision must, of course, be made by the voters of the countries concerned. But no one should expect that this question is not of concern to this government. Whether some of the Communist parties in Western Europe are, in fact, independent of Moscow cannot be determined when their electoral self-interest so overwhelmingly coincides with their claims. Their internal procedures—their Leninist principles and dogmas—remain the antithesis of democratic parties. And were they to gain power they would do so after having advocated for decades programs and values detrimental to our traditional ties.

By that record they would inevitably give low priority to security and Western defense efforts, which are essential

not only to Europe's freedom but to maintaining the world balance of power. They would be tempted to orient their economies to a much greater extent toward the East. We would have to expect that Western European governments in which Communists play a dominant role would, at best, steer their countries' policies toward the positions of the nonaligned. The political solidarity and collective defense of the West—and thus NATO—would be inevitably weakened if not undermined. And in this country the commitment of the American people to maintain the balance of power in Europe—justified though it might be on pragmatic, geopolitical grounds—would lack the moral base on which it has stood for thirty years.

We consider the unity of the great industrial democracies crucial to all we do in the world. For this reason we have sought to expand our cooperation to areas beyond our mutual defense—in improved political consultation, in coordinating our approaches to negotiations with the East, in reinforcing our respective economic policies, in developing a common energy policy, and in fashioning common approaches for the increasingly important dialogue with the developing nations. We have made remarkable progress in all these areas. We are determined to continue. Our foreign policy has no higher priority.

This then is the design of our foreign policy:

☐ We have the military and economic power together with our allies to prevent aggression.

☐ We have the self-confidence and vision to go beyond confrontation to a reduction of tensions and ultimately a more cooperative world.

☐ We have the resources, technology, and organizational genius to build a new relationship with the developing nations.

☐ We have the moral courage to hold high, together with our allies, the banners of freedom in a turbulent and changing world.

The challenges before us are monumental. But it is not every generation that is given the opportunity to shape a new international order. If the opportunity is missed, we shall live in a world of chaos and danger. If it is realized we will have entered an era of peace and progress and justice.

But we can realize our hopes only as a united people. Our challenge—and its solution—lies in ourselves. Our greatest foreign policy problem is our divisions at home. Our greatest foreign policy need is national cohesion and a return to the awareness that in foreign policy we are all engaged in a common national endeavor.

The world watches with amazement—our adversaries with glee and our friends with growing dismay—how America seems bent on eroding its influence and destroying its achievements in world affairs through an orgy of recrimination.

They see our policies in Africa, the eastern Mediterranean, in Latin America, in East-West relations undermined by arbitrary congressional actions that may take decades to undo.

They see our intelligence system gravely damaged by unremitting, undiscriminating attack.

They see a country virtually incapable of behaving with the discretion that is indispensable for diplomacy.

They see revelations of malfeasance abroad on the part of American firms wreak grave damage on the political structures of friendly nations. Whatever wrongs were committed—reprehensible as they are—should be dealt with in a manner consistent with our own judicial procedures—and with the dignity of allied nations.

They see some critics suddenly pretending that the Soviets are ten feet tall and that America, despite all the evidence to the contrary, is becoming a second-rate nation. They know these erroneous and reckless allegations to be dangerous, because they may, if continued, persuade allies and adversaries of our weakness, tempting the one to accommodation and the other to adventurism.

They see this Administration—which has been condemned by one set of critics for its vigorous reaction to expansionism in Southeast Asia, in the Middle East, in Africa—simultaneously charged by another group of opponents with permitting unilateral Soviet gains.

They see that the Administration, whose defense budgets have been cut some $39 billion by the Congress in the past seven years, is simultaneously charged with neglecting American defenses.

The American people see all this, too, and wonder when it will end. They know that we cannot escape either our responsibilities or the geopolitical realities of the world around us. For a great nation that does not manage events will soon be overwhelmed by them.

If one group of critics undermines arms control negotiations and cuts off the prospect of more constructive ties with the Soviet Union while another group cuts away at our defense budgets and intelligence services and thwarts American resistance to Soviet adventurism, both combined will—whether they have intended it or not—end by wrecking the nation's ability to conduct a strong, creative, moderate, and prudent foreign policy. The result will be paralysis, no matter who wins in November. And if America cannot act, others will, and we and all the free peoples of the world will pay the price.

So our problem is at once more complex and simpler than in times past. The challenges are unprecedented but the remedies are in our own hands. This Administration has confidence in the strength, resilience, and vigor of America. If we summon the American spirit and restore our unity, we will have a decisive and positive impact on a world which, more than ever, affects our lives and cries out for our leadership.

Those who have faith in America will tell the American people the truth:

☐ That we are strong and at peace;

☐ That there are no easy or final answers to our problems;

☐ That we must conduct a long-term and responsible foreign policy, without escape and without respite;

☐ That what is attainable at any one moment will inevitably fall short of the ideal;

☐ That the reach of our power and purpose has its limits;

☐ That nevertheless we have the strength and determination to defend our interests and the conviction to uphold our values; and finally

☐ That we have the opportunity to leave our children a more cooperative, more just, and more peaceful world than we found.

In this Bicentennial year we celebrate ideals which began to take shape around the shores of Massachusetts Bay some 350 years ago. We have accomplished great things as a united people; there is much yet to do. This country's work in the world is not a burden but a triumph—and the measure of greatness yet to come.

Americans have always made history rather than let history chart our course. We, the present generation of Americans, will do no less. So let this year mark the end of our divisions. Let it usher in an era of national reconciliation and rededication by all Americans to their common destiny. Let us have a clear vision of what is before us—glory and danger alike—and go forward together to meet it.

# WORLDWIDE AMNESTY FOR POLITICAL PRISONERS [3]

## Daniel P. Moynihan [4]

In an article in *Commentary* (March 1975, p. 42), Daniel P. Moynihan declared, "It is time that . . . the American spokesman came to be feared in the international forums for the truths he might tell." In the seven months (July through January) while he served as the United States ambassador to the United Nations, Moynihan put into practice his bold declaration. Rather than use the expected diplomatic double talk he spoke frankly and forthrightly and at times shocked the diplomatic community.

When the UN Assembly approved a report of its Decolonization Committee charging that US bases were maintained in the Virgin Islands to menace Latin American and Caribbean nations, Moynihan called the United Nations a "theater of the absurd." Before the AFL-CIO Constitutional Convention, San Francisco, October 3, 1975, he branded Uganda's President, Idi Amin, who had called for the "elimination of Israel as a state" as a "racist murderer." But perhaps his most fierce rhetoric was leveled at the General Assembly when it voted 72 to 35 for a resolution equating Zionism with racism. He called the measure "an obscene act" and said that the United States, "does not acknowledge, it will not abide by, it will never acquiesce in this infamous act."

Moynihan's hard-hitting, stark rhetoric surprised the UN diplomatic observers. The Third World diplomats viewed his statements as "opportunistic," "arrogant," and "outrageous" (*Wall Street Journal,* January 12, 1976). Ivor Richard of Great Britain likened him to "Wyatt Earp looking for shootouts in the OK Corral" (New York *Times,* February 3, 1976). Rumors circulated that Secretary of State Henry Kissinger was embarrassed by the Moynihan statements and his confrontation with diplomats from the Third World and Communist countries. In contrast, the American public viewed their UN ambassador as a "breath of fresh air." An opinion poll released in December showed that 70 percent of the Americans questioned approved of Moynihan's frankness and thought that he should continue to speak "frankly

[3] Delivered to Committee III of the General Assembly, United Nations, New York City, November 12, 1975.
[4] For biographical note, see Appendix.

and forthrightly." Only 16 percent thought that he should be more diplomatic and tactful (Baton Rouge *State Times,* February 1, 1976).

On November 12, 1975, Moynihan proposed to Committee III of the General Assembly (social, humanitarian, and cultural questions) that all nations grant amnesty to political prisoners. This committee is one of seven through which the General Assembly channels its work. All member nations (143 at the time of the speech) have seats and their representatives meet in the committee of the whole to do the business of the Assembly. On the day of the speech, most of the representatives—a vast majority—were present. With an obvious strategy, Moynihan sought to embarrass those persons who two days before had voted for a resolution equating Zionism with racism (*Newsweek,* November 24, 1975). His purpose was to expose the hypocrisy of Third World and Communist nations for condemning Israel and at the same time holding in jails thousands of political prisoners.

Responding with considerable debate and parliamentary maneuvering, the opposition attempted to kill the thrust of the proposal through the process of amendment. As a result Leonard Garment, the United States representative on the Human Rights Commission, withdrew the proposal November 21, 1975, and explained the position of the United States:

> For since we introduced this resolution, no fewer than fifteen amendments to it have been submitted. Almost all of those amendments are formulated with farfetched analogies, lacking in minimal juridical sensibility, and designed to turn this resolution into a meaningless gesture or worse; certainly an act that has no place in the forum in which we are assembled.

> Predictably, these fifteen amendments are in effect but one, each pointing in the same direction as if the product of a common plan. Not one is primarily concerned with people held in prison, merely for thinking or expressing thoughts discomforting to their governments; indeed, almost all of them make absolutely no reference to such prisoners. These amendments are devoid of any concern for the danger faced by these men and women who are like prisoners of war, captives in the hands of their enemies. . . .

> When we took this step, we asked this body to join its voice in asking that the world open the doors of its political jails so that perhaps some day it will open the doors and break down the walls that keep men and women from enjoying

life in places of their own choosing. As we withdraw this resolution, we do so not out of a sense of final defeat, but with the hope that over time this request will be answered. In that hope we will persist.

The Moynihan speech as a counterdiplomatic move had a subtle purpose that is difficult to analyze. What response did the speaker hope for? Was he serious in his proposal? Did he have any reason to believe that his speech would result in action? Or was he playing a diplomatic game? Quite obviously Moynihan aimed at an audience much wider than that assembled at the United Nations. Probably he hoped to encourage oppressed millions who struggle with tyranny. On December 2, 1975, he addressed the Pacem in Terris IV Convocation sponsored by the Center for the Study of Democratic Institutions. (*Pacem in Terris* is an encyclical of Pope John XXIII issued in 1963, presenting and interpreting the natural-law principles that govern the political order.) In this address Moynihan elaborated on his diplomatic purposes:

Already, we hear voices from the other world asking for truth. From us. About them. Most particularly, and most poignantly, we hear voices from the Soviet Union which ask no more than *Pacem in Terris* commands: that as between governments and their respective peoples "it is not fear which should reign but love. . . ."

That is our strength: that we can say this, and that the nations with which we are leagued can say it. Those who cannot say it must perforce hear it from us with ever mounting concern, a concern which they will attempt to allay by measures which will only enhance that concern.

Surely we must see this. Just as we must see the persistent attempt to dissuade us from speaking out for what it is: the assertion of their weakness and our strength. The night the American amnesty resolution was introduced, a German newspaperwoman called on me, an appointment made several weeks earlier. As we sat down she said, "Before beginning, let me just tell you that already the news of what the United States has proposed will be whispered from cell to cell in East German prisons. You would think such news would never reach such places, but it does and it is what keeps you alive. I know. I spent four years in one of them." On the heels of our initiative, one American commentator, having declared us unworthy to do anything decent, gleefully predicted that our effort would be met with a "deadly silence." Which in retrospect might to many seem

to be the case. But is it the case? Or is it only that we
have not learned to hear the whispers?

Mr. Chairman, my delegation rises to address the Third
Committee in a matter which may be the most important
social, cultural and humanitarian proposal which the
United States has made in very many years and which we
regard as one of the most important which this Committee
will ever have had before it.

In an address on the occasion of the thirtieth anniversary of the United Nations, United States Secretary of State
Henry A. Kissinger took note that we are living at one of
the rarest moments in the modern history of the world. For
at this moment, in all of the world, there is not a single
nation-state engaged in war against another nation-state.

It appears to the United States that such a moment invites—calls for—no less extraordinary measures of reconciliation not only between nations, but within them. To this
end, the United States desires to propose a world-wide amnesty for political prisoners. It proposes a General Assembly
resolution which

> Appeals to all governments to proclaim an uncondi-
> tional amnesty by releasing all political prisoners in the
> sense of persons deprived of their liberty primarily because
> they have, in accordance with the Universal Declaration of
> Human Rights, sought peaceful expression of beliefs and
> opinions at variance with those held by their governments
> or have sought to provide legal or other forms of nonviolent
> assistance to such persons.

The United Nations has, in truth, already taken, at this
General Assembly, at least two steps in this direction.

□ A draft resolution in the Special Political Committee,
entitled Solidarity With the South African Political Prisoners, calls on "South Africa to grant an unconditional amnesty to all persons imprisoned or restricted for their opposition to apartheid or acts arising from such opposition. . . ."

The United States voted for this resolution.

☐ A draft resolution in the Social, Cultural, and Humanitarian Committee, entitled Protection of Human Rights in Chile, called for the government there to ensure "The rights of all persons to liberty and security of person, in particular those who have been detained without charge or in prison solely for political reasons."

The United States voted for this resolution.

Is there, however, any reason to stop there, to limit our concerns to only two members of the United Nations, when there are all together 142 members? The resolution on Protection of Human Rights in Chile declares, *inter alia,* that "No one shall be held guilty of any criminal offense on account of any act or omission which did not constitute a criminal offense under national or international law at the time when it was committed. . . ." It has to be noted that more and more international pronouncements of this kind declare that there are crimes in international law for which individuals may be held responsible. Similarly, it is more and more held that there are actions against individuals for which governments may be held responsible, at least in the sense that they are expected not to take such actions. The exact state of the law in this area is not one on which there will be universal agreement. Yet, clearly, something akin to common law rights is emerging in international law which protects individuals where "universally condemned" or "abhorrent" actions are involved. It is to these standards that Secretary Kissinger appealed in his address to the General Assembly, earlier in this session, when he raised the issue of torture. Torture, he said, is

> . . . a practice which all nations should abhor. It is an absolute debasement of the function of government when its overwhelming power is used, not for people's welfare but as an instrument of their suffering.

Now it follows from these considerations that even as South Africa and Chile are obliged by certain standards con-

cerning prisoners, for example, so equally are all other members of the United Nations. It is implicitly acknowledged, however, that it is for governments themselves to conform to international standards. And if some governments, then all governments.

Hence, at this moment, the singular appeal of amnesty. A moment of peace and of peacemaking, and a mode which allows governments to do what they ought without the appearance of coercion. All governments.

Universality in this matter is of special concern to the United States government—and we would hope to all governments. There are two grounds for this concern which strike us with special force.

The *first* is that the selective morality of the United Nations in matters of human rights threatens the integrity not merely of the United Nations, but of human rights themselves. There is no mystery in this matter. Unless standards of human rights are seen to be applied uniformly and neutrally to all nations, regardless of the nature of their regimes or the size of their armaments, unless this is done, it will quickly be seen that it is not human rights at all which are invoked when selective applications are called for, but simply arbitrary political standards dressed up in the guise of human rights. From this perception it is no great distance to the conclusion that in truth there are no human rights recognized by the international community.

A generation ago the British poet Stephen Spender came to this perception in the course of visits to Spain during its long and tragic civil war. He had first come to Spain out of sympathy for one of the sides in that heartrending conflict. He had returned to England to report what he had seen of atrocities committed by the other side. Thereafter he made several trips to Spain, over the course of which he was forced to realize that atrocities were not a monopoly of one side only; they were indeed all too common on both sides. At which point, to his great and lasting honor, he wrote: "It came to me that unless I cared about every murdered

child indiscriminately, I didn't really care about children being murdered at all."

This is what the United States proposal is about. Unless we care about political prisoners everywhere, we don't really care about them anywhere. It is something else altogether that is on our minds, something we conceal with the language of human rights, in the course of which we commence to destroy that language, much as George Orwell, who fought in the Spanish Civil War, saw that it would be destroyed.

Our concern about discriminatory treatment is not eased by scrutiny of the list of cosponsors of the draft resolutions on South Africa and Chile. These are, to repeat, resolutions calling attention to the plight of political prisoners. The South African draft resolution has sixty cosponsors. The Chilean draft resolution has thirty-three. The United States has broken down these respective lists according to "The Comparative Survey of Freedom," that great contribution to clear thinking and plain speaking which is the work of Freedom House, an American institution of impeccable credentials, which traces its beginnings to the first efforts in the United States to win support for the nations then engaged in the mortal struggle against nazism and fascism in Europe. "The Comparative Survey of Freedom" ranks the levels of political rights and civil rights in individual nations on a scale of 1 to 7, and then gives a general summary ranking "Status of Freedom," by which nations are classified as Free, Partly Free, or Not Free. One of the melancholy attributes of a nation judged Not Free is that, in the opinion of the distinguished political scientists who carry out this survey, the nation is one in which individuals are imprisoned for political beliefs or activities of a noncriminal nature. In other words a nation with political prisoners.

What does "The Comparative Survey of Freedom" tell us about the cosponsors of these resolutions? It tells us that in its judgment, no fewer than twenty-three of the cospon-

sors of the draft resolution calling for amnesty for South African political prisoners, have political prisoners of their own. In the case of the draft resolution calling attention to the plight of political prisoners in Chile, it would appear that sixteen of the cosponsors fall into the category of nations which have political prisoners of their own.

This leads to a particularly disturbing thought about the processes by which the United Nations has come to be so concerned about human rights in some countries, but not in others. This is that we tend to know about violations of freedom—know at the time and in detail—only in those countries which permit *enough* freedom for internal opposition to make its voice heard when freedoms are violated.

This is the case, is it not, in South Africa, where there are said to be over one hundred political prisoners. For it is not necessary to *go* to South Africa to learn of violations of human rights there. One need only subscribe to the South African press, a press which while no doubt curbed in some ways, or even many ways, is nonetheless capable of frontal assault on the policies of the South African government.

The Cape *Times,* for example, in its lead editorial of November 3 states, referring to an act that has been taking place here in the General Assembly by the United States government:

> The controversy over detentions and opposition to apartheid between South Africa and the United States is unfortunate for it could harm the Republic's chances of establishing a firmer foothold on world opinion at a critical time. It also illustrates how indefensible the present system of detention is in South Africa. The fact is that unless Mr. Vorster is prepared to reveal reasons for detentions, he will be unable to answer convincingly the United States government charge that people are detained whose only act is outspoken opposition to apartheid. To term this a "downright lie" as Mr. Vorster has, might sound impressive for domestic consumption, but it is not really satisfactory.

The editorial concludes, and I have the honor to be asso-

ciated here with my distinguished friend, Mr. Clarence Mitchell, about which this editorial is being wrtten:

> For a start, Mr. Vorster should abolish the iniquitous terrorism act if he wants to deal effectively with the US charge. The act provides for indefinite detention incommunicado and without trial, on the mere say-so of a police officer. There are no effective judicial reviews or guarantees. While the system remains on the statute books, charges such as the recent US delegate's remarks in the UN will persist; and they cannot be answered convincingly. South Africa, moreover, will remain in the dubious company of countries which bypass the due process of law as part of the ordinary routine.

Is it not also the case that the freedom of the press in South Africa—such as it may be, for we do not assert it to be complete—contrasts sharply with that of its neighbors? In the *Monthly Bulletin* of the International Press Institute of June 1975, Mr. Frank Barton, Africa Director of IPI, is reported as having told the Assembly of that impeccably neutral and scrupulous organization:

> The unpalatable fact is—and this is something that sticks in the throat of every self-respecting African who will face it—is that there is more press freedom in South Africa than in the rest of Africa put together.

And what of Chile, that troubled land, where at least one estimate states that there are some five thousand political prisoners, and which is rated "partly free" by the Freedom House Comparative Survey?

One of the operative paragraphs of the draft resolution on Chile, for which the United States voted,

> *Deplores* the refusal of the Chilean authorities to allow the Ad Hoc Working Group of the Commission on Human Rights to visit the country, notwithstanding previous solemn assurances. . . .

This is true. But it is only part of the truth. The whole truth would include the fact that Amnesty International and the International Red Cross *were* permitted to visit

Chile. Moreover, if the visit of the Working Group had gone through, it would have been the *first time in history* that any government had permitted such a visit.

Are we not forced to acknowledge the point made recently by Mr. Robert Moss, the editor of *The* (London) *Economist*'s Foreign Report:

> If the military regime in Chile, following the example of all self-respecting Communist revolutionaries, had flatly decided to shut out all foreign reporters . . . [and] civil rights investigators, for a period of, say, six months after the coup, our diet of horror stories from Chile would have been meager indeed.

And are we not forced to take note of the report of Milton Friedman, the distinguished American economist who recently visited Chile:

> On the atmosphere in Chile, it is perhaps not irrelevant that at two universities, the Catholic University and the University of Chile, I gave talks on the Fragility of Freedom, in which I explicitly characterized the existing regime as unfree, talked about the difficulty of maintaining a free society, the role of free markets and free enterprise in doing so, and the urgency of establishing those preconditions for freedom. There was no advance or ex post facto censorship, the audiences were large and enthusiastic, and I received no subsequent criticism.

It is not the purpose of this statement to be accusatory, or to arouse ill feeling. But is it not the case that this year we have seen any number of regimes completely or almost completely seal off their countries, barring or expelling foreign newsmen, such that at most rumor reaches the outside world as to what is going on inside?

Simple justice requires that the United States, for one, acknowledge that while we have supported resolutions critical of repressive practices of the governments both of South Africa and Chile at this General Assembly, we have done so in the company of nations whose own internal conditions are as repressive or more so.

And what of Israel, a country rated Free by Freedom House, with high if not perfect scores in Political Rights and Civil Rights? Is it not enough to say that much of the case being made against Israel by other nations today, is made in the first instance by the fully legal opposition parties within Israel, including Arab-based parties, many of which have been quite successful in electing members to public office, and that this opposition is given notable expression in the Arabic-language press in Israel which has been described as the freest Arab-language press in the world?

Thus we come to the *second* of the concerns which animate the United States at this point. This is the concern not only that the language of human rights is being distorted and perverted; it is that the language of human rights is increasingly being turned in United Nations forums against precisely those regimes which acknowledge some or all of its validity and they are not, I fear, a majority of the regimes in this United Nations. More and more the United Nations seems only to know of violations of human rights in countries where it is still possible to protest such violations.

Let us be direct. If this language can be turned against one democracy, why not all democracies? Are democracies not singular in the degree to which at all times voices will be heard protesting this injustice or that injustice? If the propensity to protest injustice is taken as equivalent to the probability that injustice does occur, then the democracies will fare poorly indeed.

And it is precisely this standard which more and more appears among us, albeit in various disguises. In 1971, for example, the World Social Report presented to the General Assembly was virtually a totalitarian document—you know of which I speak. I was in this Committee at that time and I said so at that time. The fundamental premise on which the assessment of social conditions in respective countries was made was that the absence of social protest indicated

the absence of social wrong. Hence, without exception, the police states of the world were judged most in the right.

Americans, and those who have studied the history of the United States, will perhaps recall the memorable image which Abraham Lincoln once used in a speech given in 1858, which we have come to call his "Framing Timbers Speech." He was protesting what he judged to be the overall purpose being served by many seemingly unrelated legislative measures of the time—the purpose of extending slavery into our western territories. (For the history of freedom in the United States is hardly without blemish.) Lincoln spoke of a "concert" of behavior:

> We cannot absolutely know that all these adaptations are the result of preconcert. But when we see a lot of framed timbers, different portions of which we know have been gotten out at different times and places and by different workmen . . . and we see these timbers joined together, and see they exactly make the frame of a house or a mill, all the tenons and mortices exactly fitting, and all the lengths and proportions of the different pieces exactly adapted to their respective places, and not a piece too many or too few— not omitting even scaffolding—or, if a single piece be lacking, we see the place in the frame exactly fitted and prepared yet to bring such piece in—in such a case, we find it impossible not to believe that . . . all understood one another from the beginning, and all worked upon a common plan or draft drawn up before the first blow was struck.

The United States makes no such assertion at this time. But it reserves the right to judge, in the months and years ahead, that there has indeed been a "plan or draft" involved in all the multifarious activities at the United Nations concerning human rights which with nigh inhuman consistency seem always, somehow, to be directed towards nations at least somewhat more free than most members of the UN, and which now most recently have been directed toward a democratic society that is unquestionably free. We reserve the right to learn that our worst suspicions have been confirmed. But in the hope that we will not be, we here and

now declare what our suspicions are. Our suspicions are that there could be a design to use the issue of human rights to undermine the legitimacy of precisely those nations which still observe human rights, imperfect as that observance may be.

To those members of the United Nations who would allay our suspicions we make this simple appeal: Join us in support of our draft resolution calling for amnesty for all political prisoners. The list of known prisoners, a list assembled by organizations such as Amnesty International, is a sufficiently long and harrowing one. But there is far more horror to be felt at the thought of the names we do *not* know. It is time to free these men and women. The time for this amnesty is past due, and the path is long. Let us take the first step here and now.

# ON HISTORY, POLITICAL ECONOMY, AND VIETNAM [7]

## JOHN KENNETH GALBRAITH [8]

On May 30, 1975, John Kenneth Galbraith, the Paul M. Warburg Professor of Economics Emeritus at Harvard University, received the Frank E. Seidman Distinguished Award in Political Economy at Memphis State University, Memphis, Tennessee. The award carries with it an honorarium of ten thousand dollars and is given "to an economist who has distinguished himself or herself by contributing internationally, in the judgment of his or her peers, to the interdisciplinary advancement of economic thought as it applies to the implementation of public policy." L. William Seidman, economic adviser to President Ford, made the presentation in honor of his father, the late Frank E. Seidman. In 1974 Gunnar Karl Myrdal had received the award.

In response to receiving the recognition Professor Galbraith, economist, educator, author, political activist, social critic, and former ambassador, gave "the acceptance paper" to the approximately 175 guests from business, government, and academia, assembled at a formal banquet at Memphis State University. He was introduced by Professor Martin Bronfenbrenner, then vice president of the American Economic Association.

Galbraith, who is six feet eight inches tall, is described as stooped "from force of habit" and as "lean and angular." He has graying brown hair and a "liturgical face." In addition to being a teacher and a prolific writer, he has had a variety of political experience, serving in numerous government posts and as Ambassador Extraordinary and Plenipotentiary to India (1961-1963) under John F. Kennedy. He served as a speech writer and adviser to Adlai Stevenson in 1952 and 1956 and to John F. Kennedy in 1960. He is reported to have written a first draft of Kennedy's memorable inaugural address (*Current Biography,* May 1975).

In a most appropriate introduction, Galbraith expressed his gratitude for the honor bestowed upon him. His presentation was

[7] Delivered at acceptance of the Frank E. Seidman Distinguished Award in Political Economy, Memphis State University, May 30, 1975. The award was established by Mr. and Mrs. P. K. Seidman in memory of Frank E. Seidman. Printed by permission of John Kenneth Galbraith and Arthur A. Bayer, director. Originally published by P. K. Seidman Foundation, March 1976.

[8] For biographical note, see Appendix.

a thoughtful analysis of why the United States failed in the Vietnam adventure. He set forth the basis of his presentation when he said, "A better historical sense would have rewards going well beyond economics; it would also improve our view of the present problems of our foreign policy." The reader should notice how the speaker inductively developed his subject, reviewing first the unsuccessful attempts of imperialism to dominate other people, and then applying the lessons of history to the experience of the United States in Vietnam. Some persons may disagree with his line of thought, but it is obvious that Galbraith served a useful function as critic of the recent involvement in Southeast Asia.

The paper was an excellent example of the superior academic lecture so much a part of the university atmosphere. It measured up to what Robert M. Hutchins referred to as "the level of critical consciousness." Hutchins explained his ideal as follows:

> To attain full humanity is to reach the level of critical consciousness. This means understanding reality and understanding that men can and should transform it. The university is that institution which should lead in the achievement of critical consciousness. It must use and contain within it all the major modes of understanding and transforming reality. Thus the university would represent and constitute the circle of knowledge, in which everything is understood in the light of everything else. (From "A Learning Society," published in REPRESENTATIVE AMERICAN SPEECHES, 1971-1972, p 161-71.)

My memory extends to few such pleasant occasions as this. Pleasant and also without anxiety. When, on rare occasions in the past, I have found myself the recipient of some similar, if lesser, honor, I have always wondered how I should compose my face. A look of modesty should obviously be combined with one of rapt appreciation. It is not an easy expression to achieve; appreciation looks very much like self-appreciation; one must practice carefully before a mirror. But tonight there is no such need. My earlier honors have been without pecuniary emolument, as delicately some would call it. So handsome is yours that the right expression comes naturally and without effort. It is one of gratitude combined with fully requited avarice. There is a line from FitzGerald after Omar that might be appropriate —perhaps all too appropriate—here:

> Some for the Glories of this World, and some
> Sigh for the Prophet's Paradise to come;
> Ah, take the Cash, and let the Credit go,
> Nor heed the rumble of a distant Drum!

You have honored me for work, real or alleged, in political economy and by that I am especially pleased. In modern times power has become increasingly a force in economic life—in the setting of prices and wages, in the resulting distribution of income, in, needless to say, the resolution of issues between the private economy and the state. The modern corporation and the modern trade union are instruments for the exercise of economic power. While these have been burgeoning, economics has been increasingly excluding their power from its purview. Increasingly economics has become a lesser branch of applied mathematics; what cannot be handled by the mathematics must be excluded by assumption. Power, to a singular degree, is one of those things. Purpose and relevance in modern economic theory have thus become subordinate to method. People who dissent from the dominant intellectual currents of their subject or time have a tendency to see themselves as somewhat larger than in life, to see others through the reverse end of the telescope. No doubt that is true of those of us who see power, including political power, as a part of economics—who rejoice in being called political economists. But there is more than vanity and foible here. Undoubtedly we are also right.

I have wished often in recent times that a disciplined preoccupation with power and the institutions for its exercise might also extend to an equally disciplined concern with history. The two, indeed, must go together. I've had occasion in the last two or three years to read rather more of Marxist theory than for a long time previously. It hasn't made me a Marxist; but I have been impressed again with the vastly superior historical sense of the social theory that is in this tradition.

A better historical sense would have rewards going well beyond economics; it would also improve our view of the present problems of our foreign policy. We have been treating our recent misfortunes as though they were unique —a special manifestation of a peculiarly American aberration. They are, in fact, another episode in a long and remarkably consistent historical experience—that of variously motivated adventure by countries which presume to higher wisdom and culture in lands distant from their own.

It is now just under nine hundred years since Western Europeans began extending the beneficence of their presence to the lesser races without the law. Then, as still, they saw themselves as the custodians of higher civilized values, the progenitors and evangelists of these values. The first effort was, of course, the First Crusade, the beginning of an enterprise which continued, though with diminishing enthusiasm, for the next four hundred years. Repeatedly during all that time it was reported back to Rome that there was light at the end of the tunnel. The Kingdom of Jerusalem, first gained and soon lost, would be redeemed. Since 1096, Austrians, Spaniards, French, British, Dutch, Belgians, Swedes, Danes, Russians, Germans, Portuguese and Italians have answered the call to a civilizing mission beyond their borders. The urge among non-Europeans has been shared by Arabs, Mongols, Turks, Japanese and Americans. Few tendencies have been for so long, so persistently a feature of human behavior.

All of these efforts over all of these nine centuries have had three features in common. All, as noted, have avowed some spiritual, cultural, moral or other civilized benefit for the people toward whom the effort was directed. All have involved, often with some tactful disguise, some element of economic interest for the country extending the benefit. And all without exception have ended in failure. In the end, there has always been rejection of the beneficiating and self-beneficiating power.

The combination of high purpose and lower economic

interest has been remarkably constant. The Crusaders, as
every schoolchild knows, were to protect the Eastern Christians from the Turks and to redeem Jerusalem from the in-
fidel. But Urban II, preaching the First Crusade in Cler-
mont in 1095, did not omit to mention that there was a lot
of excellent land in that part of the world only awaiting
occupation by the Christians. As men knelt to take the
cross, there was a companion obeisance to the thought of
good real estate. Similarly the Spaniards combined a concern for extending the sway of Christ and the Holy Catholic
Church with an even more compelling interest in increasing
their cash reserves of silver and gold. The British sought to
bring the rule of law, the benefits of sound government to
Indians and Africans while bringing the trade of these peoples to London, Liverpool and Bristol. The French sought
to extend the beneficent and enduring values of French
culture; they combined this with economic objectives similar to those of the British, although less thoughtfully pursued. The American aim in Puerto Rico and the Philippines
was deemed wholly selfless and benign and exclusively to
assist subject peoples suddenly, almost accidentally liberated
from Spain. But it is not without importance that these
islands were soon extensively covered with sugar planta-
tions, mostly under continental ownership. Save by a
sycophantic minority that allied itself socially, politically
or culturally with the paramount power, this civilizing effort was rarely appreciated, even when the motives were
exceptionally pure, even when by some objective standard
the rule was better than whatever preceded it. Notable
among the Crusaders were the two orders of armed monks—
the Knights Templar and the Knights of St. John of the
Hospital. None stirred more resentment than the Templars.
This had much to do with their high religious profession,
especially as it was combined with a powerful commitment
to lending money at exorbitant rates of interest. India, in
the last century, was an exceedingly well-governed country.
In efficiency, honesty, stability, safety of person and prop-

erty, administration, it was a quantum step on from the contentious, corrupt, petty and predacious despotisms that it replaced. To this day what was British India—that governed directly by the British Raj—is perceptibly more prosperous than that which was governed indirectly through the princes—the Nabobs, the Nizam, the Rajahs and the Maharajahs. This was not forgiven.

One of the rare pleasures of serving in India in my time was the informal, unstructured and wholly fascinating conversations which Jawaharlal Nehru invited on a wide variety of subjects of no official interest to either of us. Once I asked him what would have been the optimal date for the British to have left India in a perfectly arranged world. He exploded in superbly contrived anger: "They had no business ever being in our country. Who asked them to come?" I reminded him that the government, so-called, that they had found had scarcely been a blessing for the average cultivator, that even ardent Indian nationalists conceded that the British in the eighteenth century were regarded as liberators in Bengal. Nehru conceded the point and compromised by saying they should certainly have been gone by the end of the first World War. In the last thousand years Alaska and Hawaii seem to be the only significant communities that have accepted government from a great distance without complaint. And now one reads of an incipient independence movement in Alaska.

It is in light of this history that the recent American experiences should be viewed. It is equally useful for understanding the post–World War II Soviet experience in Yugoslavia, China, Czechoslovakia, Algeria and Egypt, but we should set a higher store by our own enlightenment. We did not, after World War II, seek directly to govern people distant from our shores. Like the Soviets we were too wise for that. We even proclaimed our aversion to colonial rule. But no less than the colonial powers we sought to guide the political and economic development of other lands. No less than the colonial powers we sought to shape these develop-

ments to our own preference, which is to say our own image.

Our technique bore a more than superficial resemblance to that of Britain in the princely states of India—to what, in a less ambiguous age, was called indirect rule. In Indochina, happily the extreme and hence the somewhat exceptional case, we supported rulers of our preference if not our choice. We worried, as did the British, about their behavior. On occasion as the paramount power we dismissed them if they were too bad. (Our standards were, however, more tolerant than those of the Raj; once in Junagadh state in Western India it dismissed an animal-loving Nabob for staging an unduly elaborate wedding between two dogs named Roshana and Bobby. About 50,000 attended the ceremony, not counting the dogs. The Prince's kennels at the time were absorbing some 10 percent of the revenues of the state which the British thought a bit high.) We surrounded our Nabobs with advisers—Lodge, Taylor, Bunker, Graham Martin. These were the modern, though decidedly more permissive, equivalent of the British Resident. We armed our men against their indigenous enemies and like the British supplied supporting force of our own. We further sought their fealty, if not in the case of General Thieu their enduring gratitude, by providing massive subsidies. We did depart from the British model in one respect. They spoke of colonialism; we said that we were securing the independence of the people in question.

In keeping with the nine-hundred-year history there was the admixture of idealism and economic interest. Nearly all the Americans giving guidance to our Indochina adventure felt, we may be sure, that they were acting in the interest of the people of that country. Freedom—freedom from the discipline and the coercion that few deny is a feature of Communist administration—was believed genuinely important.

As to the companion economic interest, I've never found much substance to the thought that our plunge into Viet-

nam was to enhance the profits of American corporations. They were doing quite well without it. The stock market invariably went up on news of peace. I spent much of 1968 raising money for the antiwar campaign of Eugene Mc-Carthy. By far the largest part of our support came from businessmen, the largest contributors being in Wall Street. But present in all postwar policy was one plank—avowed or unavowed. To preserve free enterprise in the United States you must act to preserve it everywhere else. Let other countries succumb to communism and who could tell that our system would survive. It was a proposition that was without merit. What happens in Vietnam has no appreciable bearing on what happens in Europe or the United States. Whether a poor rural society calls itself Communist or capitalist does not make much difference. It is a poor, rural society in either case. Only a very sensitive ideologist, walking through a Laotian jungle, can tell whether it is a free-enterprise jungle or a Socialist jungle. But this is not the point. We had persuaded ourselves of our interest.

In keeping with all the history, we have been rejected. In light of this history—the history of the effort of people to give government or even guidance to others that are ethnically, culturally or geographically distant—we should hardly be surprised.

You will ask why, in relation to Hanoi, the Chinese and Russians did better. One answer is that they were wiser: No Chinese or Russian troops were sent; no large body of advisers debouched; there was a Pentagon East but no Kremlin East. To this day we do not know which country, China or the Soviet Union, was most influential in North Vietnam.

We do know that where the Soviet influence and presence have been strong the experience has not been different from our own. In Yugoslavia, China, Algeria, Egypt, the Soviets have also had the experience, in the language of my Vermont neighbors, of being thrown out. I once asked a Soviet journalist what they did with their failed Yugo-

slav, Albanian, Chinese, Egyptian and other like strategists. Did they, following our humane practice, go back to teach the young? Were they available for thoughtful seminars at some Bolshevist equivalent of the Council on Foreign Relations? Did they explain how it all happened on the Op-Ed page of *Pravda?* He replied only: "We have them."

The Indochina experience, however regarded, was a tragedy. Voltaire killed off Dr. Pangloss rather early in his academic career; it was a wise decision, and we should all deplore the recent efforts to revive him and put him on the White House payroll. But there are two aspects of our Indochina experience which are not altogether dark. One even is encouraging. There is a well-articulated view on the left that what happened in Indochina is inevitable under capitalism. It reflects that uncontrollable imperialist drive—the drive for markets, for outlets for investment, for justification for military spending and power. We see that inability to be guided by historical experience was far more plausibly the cause. Those responsible were not the helpless instruments of a capitalist dynamic. They were men of limited vision who did not know the limits of their vision.

The men responsible for Vietnam were themselves an historical accident. They came to office when foreign policy was a fashionable pursuit of the Establishment, when it basked in the prestige of World War II and its aftermath, when a principal qualification was no excessive identification with liberal or left-wing politics and a negative saliva test on anything that might suggest sympathy for communism. The most elementary of political propositions—that men will not rally to the support of rascals, would not die to sustain the greed of others—was well beyond the perception of the men so selected. I speak with some personal animus here. There were a number of us who made this case. We encountered that peculiarly refined contempt of the self-styled practical man for what he cannot understand and does not wish to understand.

Foolishness is not a minor problem in our time. But it

is not inherent in our system. We are not impelled to its practice. It could be remediable. In this case there was remedy. It came, let us note, from the system—it came out of the good sense of the country as a whole. It is in this that we can justly take the satisfaction. When before has a great country stopped in the middle of a war, assessed the wisdom of its participation, decided it was wrong, asserted this judgment against all of the chauvinist tendencies aroused by military conflict, and brought its participation to an end? The answer is never. You will say that in Vietnam and Algeria the French followed a similar course. We, unlike the French, had a choice. Surely there were elements of greatness in the way the nation corrected the error of its leaders on Vietnam. I wish more of our people, including more of our critics abroad, might take note of this achievement. Does it not say something for democracy?

However, let us not make the presence of this remedial power a license for any more such errors.

Thank you very much again.

# PERSISTENT PROBLEMS AT HOME

## UNFINISHED BUSINESS [1]

### VERNON E. JORDAN JR.[2]

In the context of the recent past, no year has been more destructive to the progress of blacks than 1975. Though it can be argued with complete justification that other Americans also sustained losses during the year, what has to be recognized is that blacks lost more and every loss represented a major setback from which it will take them years to recover.

America should not make the mistake of believing that because the problems of blacks and the poor did not have high visibility or command public attention in 1975 that they no longer exist, or have been ameliorated to such an extent they are no longer important.

The problems remain. They grew worse in 1975.

The statement cited above is the evaluation of the National Urban League concerning the plight of blacks at present. It was issued January 22, 1976. "The last to be hired and the first to be fired" has been too often true. Poverty, hunger, disillusionment, and unemployment are always present in black ghettos. These conditions gave urgency to the speaking of Vernon Jordan Jr., executive director of the National Urban League.

Vernon E. Jordan had a unique experience when he addressed a joint session of the General Assembly of South Carolina, Columbia, Wednesday, March 10, 1976. Not too long before, whites had vigorously resisted integration of any type. Now this prominent black spokesman was invited by joint resolution coming from black and white legislators to appear in the state capitol. Close by are many reminders of the South's past. Nearby are statues of Wade Hampton, Ben Tillman, and John C. Calhoun. In the lobby engraved in marble is the 1860 secession declaration. Hanging over the rostrum of the General Assembly are three flags: the United States flag, the flag of South Carolina, and the Stars and Bars of the Confederacy.

[1] Delivered at a joint session of the General Assembly of South Carolina, Columbia, March 10, 1976. Title supplied by editor. Quoted by permission.
[2] For biographical note, see Appendix.

There was a striking parallel between Jordan's appearance and that of Booker T. Washington, who addressed the Atlanta Exposition, September 18, 1895, over eighty years before. In the case of Washington, it was "the first time in the entire history of the Negro that a member of [his] race had been asked to speak from the same platform with white southern men and women" (*Up From Slavery*, p 148). Jordan was the first black civil rights leader ever to be invited to speak before the General Assembly of South Carolina. Jordan had been reared in Georgia and not long before had helped desegregate the University of Georgia. He was correct in observing that his presence in South Carolina was "indeed symbolic of the giant strides toward maturity and toward interracial cooperation we have made here in the South." The passing of eighty years between the two occasions was also symbolic of the obstinacy of racial antagonisms.

Worthy of thought are the contrasts between Washington and Jordan. The first significant black educator came as an accommodator, willing to agree to the inferior status of his race, but arguing for acceptance of the black as a valuable worker and for improvement of the status of blacks. He told his white listeners what they wanted to hear. On the other hand, Jordan, perhaps the most articulate spokesman for blacks in the United States, came as an equal to make a fervent appeal for improvement in employment and economic well-being of the poor, including blacks. Washington probably addressed an audience predominantly from Georgia, hoping, of course, to impress northern philanthropists who donated funds to his school at Tuskegee. Jordan, head of a powerful lobby group, had a forthright message for his immediate listeners, but he also was much more interested in a national audience, particularly Congress.

Noticeable in the speech was one strong southern appeal, often directed to southern self-consciousness. The southern advocate has often suggested that because the "southern way of life" is morally superior to that of other sections, the South is destined to set the example for others to follow. With disturbing reports of racial violence over busing coming from Boston and other northern cities, Jordan was assured of approval and endorsement when he said:

It is the South, above all other regions, that can teach our fellow Americans of the futility of racism, the evils of economic exploitation, and the necessity for positive, constructive change. It is the South that can bring a humanizing influence to bear on the new technology and new industrial development. It is the South whose unique history

can demonstrate to the rest of the nation the value of racial reconciliation and partnerships.

Whether the South will do this, or whether it will be content to become just another section, indistinguishable from the others, depends in large part upon its continued progress in race relations and upon its ability to include black people as full economic equals. It depends on what this Assembly and others like it in the South do about issues at the state level that directly affect the well being and the opportunities of black citizens.

Jordan, who is six feet four inches tall and weighs over two hundred pounds, is a speaker with a commanding presence. On the platform or before television cameras he suggests dignity and confidence. Articulate and forceful, he has many invitations to speak. For example, recently he has spoken to such groups as the 75th annual conference of the National Business League, Boston, October 10, 1975; the inaugural ceremonies of Tennessee State University, Nashville, October 24, 1975; the Institution of Human Relations, New York City, November 21, 1975; the New England Life Forum, Boston, February 4, 1976. At the spring commencements he spoke at Williams College and Notre Dame University. His speeches are frequently reprinted in the magazine *Vital Speeches of the Day* (see issues of July 1, 1975 and September 15, 1975). For two of his speeches previously printed in REPRESENTATIVE AMERICAN SPEECHES, see the compilations for 1971-1972, p 49-58, and 1972-1973, p 39-49.

I join you today in gratitude for your invitation, and deeply mindful of the historic nature of this occasion. My presence here is indeed symbolic of the giant strides toward maturity and toward interracial cooperation we have made here in the South.

Who among us would have thought a dozen years ago, that a black civil rights leader would be invited to share with this distinguished body his views on the pressing issues of our times? Who among us, years ago, could have predicted that this General Assembly would include among its distinguished membership black political leaders? And who among us in that not-too-distant past, could have foreseen the great changes in race relations that have taken place.

So, moved as I am by the personal honor bestowed upon me, I cannot but reflect on the symbolic nature of this event, and on the recognition it implies for the constructive work of the organization I represent, the National Urban League.

The National Urban League is a key institution in the black community, and in the white community as well. It provides vital community services, an advocacy voice for minority Americans, a bridge between the races, and is committed to the open, pluralistic, integrated society.

Among our 104 affiliates, I am proud to number twenty-five in the South, including the Urban leagues of Columbia and Greenville, with whose great work I hope you are familiar. The leadership of those leagues is here today—Lincoln C. Jenkins, president, and Hiram Spain, executive director of the Columbia Urban League, and from Greenville, Joseph T. Allmon, president, and William B. Whitney, executive director. These two leagues have a combined budget of over a million dollars, employ over one hundred people of both races and serve their communities with successful programs in jobs, training, counseling, education, child development and a host of other key areas.

This year we celebrate America's Bicentennial, the two hundredth anniversary of our nation's independence. It is also an election year.

It is, then, a time uniquely situated for self-examination, for redefining what America is all about, and for dealing with the unfinished business of fulfilling the American Dream, the still-to-be-completed promise embodied in our Declaration of Independence that "all men are created equal, that they are endowed by their Creator with certain unalienable rights, that among these are life, liberty and the pursuit of happiness."

Those words shine like beacons through the ages. They have inspired men in far-off countries, as they have inspired our own people. They stand today as reminders that the barriers of race, of poverty, and of joblessness should not be

tolerated in the birthplace of liberty and the fount of equality.

America's birthday celebration is tarnished because it occurs in a year of intolerably high unemployment, of rising poverty and of continued national economic recession. Thus, our Bicentennial must be the occasion not merely for self-congratulation, but for a critical appraisal of what must be done to extend our national ideals to all of our citizens. The grim reality of unequal opportunity for many millions of Americans should inspire us to positive actions to reorder our national priorities and fulfill the aspirations of all of our people.

There are today in America, over 24 million people officially classified as poor, and some estimates place the number at 40 million because the official poverty line has lagged behind rising prices.

There are today in America over 7 million people officially classified as unemployed, and if we add to them 5 million discouraged workers who have given up looking for nonexistent jobs, and over 3 million part-time workers who want full-time work, we find some 15 million people unemployed or subemployed. And that does not even include about 2 million people who work full-time for below-poverty-level wages.

Those are national statistics. Here in the South, the situation is even worse; the poverty rate, involuntary part-time work, and subemployment are all higher.

And both nationally and regionally, black people fare worse than do whites. Southern black unemployment is over double the white rate; a third of all black families are poor and half of them do not receive a single cent from welfare; earnings of black workers average only about two thirds that of whites, and in almost every measure of socioeconomic status, blacks lag behind whites and in many instances, the gap is growing, not closing.

Just as a disproportionate number of southern whites

are poor and subemployed, so too, do we find a disproportionate number of southern blacks lagging behind their
white neighbors.

Thus, southerners have a strong stake in national policies that increase employment opportunities and reduce
the shameful poverty that still stalks our land.

Despite the current popularity of optimistic predictions
about the economy, it is clear that unemployment and poverty will continue to remain at unconscionably high levels.
Administration spokesmen predict unemployment will still
be at the seven-million level by year's end and full employment is now universally regarded as unattainable.

To accept this however, is to accept continued joblessness for many millions of people who desperately want to
work, white and black alike. To accept this is to doom
those people and their children to marginal economic existence and to rob America of the full prosperity for all that
she is capable of achieving. And to accept this is to doom
ourselves to artificially-lowered living standards and to federal budget deficits.

For every million people out of work, the government
loses $16 billion in lost tax receipts and in unemployment
benefits. This year alone abnormally high unemployment
rates cost our economy over $150 billion in lost economic
growth. This year alone, the federal government will spend
over forty billion in unemployment compensation and in
welfare costs, most of which would not be necessary if we
had full employment.

If our nation had implemented a full employment policy twenty years ago we would have produced in that time
an extra 2 trillion dollars' worth of goods and services and
federal tax receipts would have gained some $500 billion.
Thus, we must ask whether we can afford *not* to have full
employment.

I would hope that this distinguished body will go on
record in support of a national full employment policy that

guarantees a decent job at a decent wage to all Americans able to work. I envision a three-pronged program to achieve this goal. It would include:

☐ Incentives to private industry to recruit, train and hire the jobless. The private sector can't do the job alone, but public policies that make it less attractive for a business to hire more workers compound the difficulty. Federal regulations, subsidies and tax incentives should all be directed at increasing the private sector's ability to create jobs.

☐ A second step would be for the federal government to create a public works program along the lines of the old WPA that helped sustain millions during the depression of the 1930s. Those public works projects lined our country with roads, with bridges, with schoolhouses and other public facilities still in use today. A similar program in the seventies would not only create jobs, but it would provide a new generation of vitally needed houses, transportation facilities and other public works our nation needs.

☐ Finally, a vastly expanded public service employment program would help fill the pressing need for public services while assuring employment opportunities for millions of people. Some years ago a presidential commission determined that public sector manpower needs in conservation, safety, education and health could accommodate some five million new jobs, offering an opportunity to sharply improve necessary public services.

A national full employment policy along the lines I have outlined here would make unemployment a thing of the past, turn revenue-consumers into producers, generate tax income to pay for itself, and remove the curse of joblessness from the land.

A national full employment policy, along with a national income-maintenance plan, would have its greatest impact right here in the South, and would go a long way

towards bringing our region to economic parity with the rest of the country.

Such a policy would not, by itself, end poverty, for there would remain those who are unable to work, who are incapable of working and thus in need of assistance that would enable them to maintain a decent living standard. The welfare system is supposed to do this, but its faults are too numerous to detail here. Everyone agrees that the welfare system is a mess, that it discourages work, penalizes the poor, and encourages dependency. It is an inconsistent patchwork of bureaucratic interference in people's lives, wildly varying benefit scales, and costly administrative charges.

But its worst fault is that it doesn't work. The welfare system for the poor is not nearly as efficient as the welfare system composed of tax loopholes and subsidies for the wealthy. That's why there is growing support for a welfare reform program that assures a liveable minimum income while relieving state and local governments of the increasing burden of providing for the needs of the poor.

I believe the most efficient reform would be a universal refundable-credit income tax that would extend a basic annual grant, or tax credit, to all. That grant would be taxable income, so that the poor would keep all of it, the near-poor would keep some of it, and middle- and upper-income families would return it all in taxes.

This system would be financed by removal of most of today's tax deductions and loopholes and the imposition of a flat tax-rate on all income. Such a system would limit subsidies to those in need, and not, as at present, to the better-off. It would supplement the incomes of working families who cannot make ends meet. And because the tax credit would be automatic and universal, it would bring big savings in administrative costs and reduce abuses so prevalent in the present system.

In fact, we have the beginnings of such a system today.

Families whose incomes are below $4,000 get a cash payment from the IRS. Those between $4,000 and $8,000 get lesser amounts.

The tax-credit route to welfare reform has attracted increasing support including key elements within the Administration. Support for federal takeover of welfare has also mounted, with several governors urging such action. It is clear that some such reform will come sooner or later, and the national nature of the problem, the continuing economic crisis confronting low-income citizens and the growing disenchantment with the present malfunctioning system all argue for sweeping reforms as soon as possible.

My proposals for a national full employment policy and for a universal refundable-credit income tax are pro-work, pro-human-dignity proposals. They would increase national productivity, stimulate the economy, end unemployment and lessen poverty. And they would go a long way toward removing the economic causes of racial antagonism.

It is too often forgotten that many more whites than blacks are jobless, are poor, and are receiving welfare. It is too often forgotten that while blacks suffer disproportionately higher rates of economic hardship, five times as many whites are jobless and twice as many are poor.

So these issues cannot be framed in racial terms; they cannot be seen solely as "black" issues. Just as more whites than blacks benefited from the social programs of the sixties, so too would more whites than blacks gain from full employment and from welfare reform.

And we should also remember that as our nation confronts an increasingly hostile world, a key element in our defense arsenal must be internal stability and economic growth. By healing the divisions within we strengthen ourselves and increase our ability to lead our friends and inspire respect in our enemies. But there is another view that says we can't afford full employment programs, income-maintenance programs, and other needed reforms. It is a view that argues that the federal government has become

too big, and that it should retreat from social and economic intervention in our society.

This view, which I call "the new minimalism," counsels a planned withdrawal from national greatness that is subversive of the ideals of equality embedded in the Declaration of Independence. And the new minimalism is wrong in its facts.

For the fact is that the federal share in the economy has not risen at all. Between 1953 and 1973 the federal budget has held steady at about 20 percent of the gross national product. The slight rise since 1973 is directly attributable to recession-related costs of unemployment compensation and welfare. That federal debt that's supposed to be so high is only about 26 percent of the GNP; back in 1950, it was an astonishing 82 percent.

Obviously, the federal government can be more responsive to the needs of its citizens and the private sector; it can be more efficient and more productive. It needs to take a hard-nosed look at costs and keep them to the minimum necessary while it also must take a hard-nosed look at national needs, and supply them to the maximum extent necessary. Just fussing at bureaucrats and at Washington won't put people to work, nor will it take us out of the cycle of boom and bust that retards our progress.

Southerners must be especially wary of the "new minimalism," for this region would be the prime beneficiary of federal job-creation programs and of federal income-maintenance programs. The economic gap between the South and the rest of the country remains, and we've got a stake in the federal responsibility to reduce that gap and to enlarge the potential of our society.

But there's another reason why southerners must be suspicious of the new minimalism, and that is because it was largely the federal initiative toward securing civil rights that has led to the true emergence of a New South, and freed us from the institutionalized racial oppression that brought terrible harm to all southerners—black and white.

Those civil rights laws that the new minimalists might cite as unwarranted federal intrusions actually provided the springboard for the region's progress. The growth of its economy, the infusion of industrial capital, and the establishment of job-producing new industries by national and international corporations could never have occurred if those corporations had to operate in the old environment of separate drinking fountains, separate public facilities and separate labor force patterns.

Yes, the South has changed; the New South is a reality, not an empty phrase, and there is a new dawn in the relations between the races. Discrimination still exists. Old patterns still survive. But I have faith that these are dying remnants of an old order that could not survive the fresh winds of the twentieth century.

When Senator Thurmond supports Matthew Perry for the Military Court of Appeals, you know there have been changes. When southern students go to Boston to counsel school bodies on how to integrate, you know there have been changes. And when a black civil rights worker from Georgia is invited to speak to you today, you know there have been changes.

Many of the changes are directly related to black voting power and to the black use of long-overdue constitutional rights. But many also derive from sincerely changed attitudes on the part of many people who, ten years ago cried "never," and who cried "interposition," "nullification," "massive resistance," and "no, not one." They have found it is easier to do right than to keep on doing wrong.

But for all the very real changes, black people remain seriously disadvantaged. It would be all too easy to become complacent, to allow highly visible or cosmetic changes to obscure the real inequities in our society. So let us restrain our enthusiasm for the fact that the worst features of the Old South have departed and let us continue to work for fulfillment of the South's potential as a beacon for the rest of a nation torn by racial divisions and economic inequities.

It is the South, above all other regions, that can teach our fellow Americans the futility of racism, the evils of economic exploitation, and the necessity for positive, constructive change. It is the South than can bring a humanizing influence to bear on the new technology and new industrial development. It is the South whose unique history can demonstrate to the rest of the nation the value of racial reconciliation and partnerships.

Whether the South will do this, or whether it will be content to become just another section, indistinguishable from the others, depends in large part upon its continued progress in race relations and upon its ability to include black people as full economic equals. It depends on what this assembly and others like it in the South do about issues at the state level that directly affect the well-being and the opportunities of black citizens. It depends on whether we come to recognize that black disadvantage is the result of special treatment for over four hundred years, and that now, a new, positive kind of special treatment is needed to make up for the past.

Lyndon Johnson said it so well just a few weeks before he died. "To be black in a white society," he said, "is not to stand on level and equal ground. While the races may stand side by side, whites stand on history's mountain and blacks stand in history's hollow. Until we overcome unequal history, we cannot overcome unequal opportunity."

Let us then, strive to overcome the unequal history we have shared these four centuries. Let us, black and white, come together in friendship and mutual respect; let us forge together a creative partnership that will make our state, our region, and our nation, a light for all mankind. Let us be mindful of our obligations to a tortured past, a difficult present, and above all, to a brighter future. Let us have faith in ourselves, in our ability to transcend the divisions of race and class and together, to build a golden, promised land for blacks and whites in our southland—a land of justice, decency and true democracy.

Yes, let us have faith. Black people have that faith. It was faith that helped us survive the harsh past and led us to become the initiator, the cutting edge, the moral force, that moved the South to change its ways and strive toward its potential for greatness.

Black people have that faith because this is our land too. We have been in South Carolina since 1526—long before the Jamestown settlement or the Pilgrims of Plymouth Rock. The first American to fall before British bullets was a black runaway slave—Crispus Attucks. Five thousand black soldiers fought side by side with white soldiers in the Revolutionary Army that won our independence.

Yes, this is our land too. This nation too often forgets that this America—this southern soil—is sprinkled with our sweat, watered with our tears, and fertilized with our blood. It too often forgets that we black people helped to build America's power and glory, that we dug the 'taters, sank the canals, toted cotton, lifted bales, and laid the railroad tracks that linked ocean to ocean.

Black people too sing "God Bless America"; we too sing of its spacious skies, its amber waves of grain; we too pledge allegiance to the flag and for what it represents. We've died in America's every war—even when we were in bondage, even when we were forced into segregated units. Our blood is on the fields of Normandy, the beaches of Iwo Jima, and the jungles of Vietnam.

Yes, this America is our land; it is the land we love, the land we have sacrificed for, the land we believe in still. Our faith in our nation is boundless. It is a faith that laments the injustices of the past and the present, but knows that the sleeping giant that is America, the great nation whose bounty and whose freedoms will one day be extended to all of its children, will awaken from its moral slumber and that black and white, together, we shall overcome.

Yes, I believe, in the eloquent words of my predecessor at the Urban League, Whitney Young:

I do have faith in America—not so much in a sudden up-surge of morality nor in a new surge toward a greater patri-otism—but I believe in the intrinsic intelligence of Ameri-cans. . . . I do not believe that we forever need to be confronted by tragedy or crises in order to act. I believe that the evidence is clear. I believe that we as a people will not wait to be embarrassed or pushed by events, into a posture of decency. I believe that America has the strength to do what is right because it is right. I am convinced that given a kind of collective wisdom and sensitivity, Americans today can be persuaded to act creatively and imaginatively to make democracy work. This is my hope, this is my dream, this is my faith.

# ENERGY AND THE JOB MARKET [3]

## JOHN C. SAWHILL [4]

We stand today no closer to a solution to our energy problem than we did during the embargo. The obvious question, then, is "Why?" Why have we failed to discipline ourselves to drive smaller, more energy-efficient automobiles, to live and work in more energy-efficient buildings, to stimulate recycling of waste materials, and to adopt other programs which would make us a more energy-conscious nation?

The answer, I believe, reflects the political stagnation in Washington—an unelected President from a minority party, and an overwhelmingly Democratic yet discouragingly undisciplined and ineffectual Congress with inept and unimaginative leadership—and all the players posturing for 1976.

In this statement Dr. John C. Sawhill, former Federal Energy Administrator (April-October 1974) and now president of New York University, assessed the energy problem of the United States.

There is little to be happy about in how the nation has met its petroleum demands. In 1973 President Richard M. Nixon launched Project Independence as a countermove to the Arab nations' oil embargo. In a rhetorical flourish he called upon the nation to dedicate itself "in this Bicentennial era" to pursue the goal of self-sufficiency in energy by 1880. Persons well-qualified in the field thought that his program was unrealistic, but they agreed that he had pointed the nation in the right direction. Months passed. Petroleum consumption increased. Domestic production decreased. World prices moved upward. The strain on the economy, both in the United States and in Europe, intensified. Oil consumers were sensitive to their precarious dependence upon the oil-producing nations. But in spite of the crisis-like atmosphere the President and Congress produced no concrete legislation.

On September 29, 1975, Dr. Sawhill addressed eight hundred persons assembled at the Middle Atlantic Placement Association,

[3] Delivered at the Middle Atlantic Placement Association Annual Fall Conference, Seven Springs Mountain Resort, Champion, Pennsylvania, September 29, 1975. Quoted by permission.
[4] For biographical note, see Appendix.

102

one of seven regional divisions of the College Placement Council, meeting at the Seven Springs Mountain Resort at Champion, Pennsylvania. In the audience were representatives from colleges and universities and recruiting officers of major corporations. The bifurcated theme of the program, "energy and the job market," gave the speaker the difficult task of establishing a connection between the two subjects. After skillfully dramatizing the implications of "the financial pressures of higher oil prices," he gave his listeners a sense of urgency when he said, "You can almost hear the time-bomb ticking."

He was particularly effective in clearly putting the crisis into terms readily understood by listeners not expert in energy problems. For example, he said "Unless we take action soon, there will be less for payrolls in America and more for bankers in Baghdad." The impact of the problem phase of the speech must have been great. The speech was a model of clarity, dramatic use of details, and adaptation to the audience.

Certainly his analysis of employment needs of the energy sector was equally well done, but the very nature of the two-pronged theme of the conference gave the speaker difficulty. Some readers may feel that the solution was not related closely enough to the speaker's dramatic presentation of the problem.

A speaker must, of course, meet the demands of the occasion and abide by the instructions of the program planner. But to do so often limits the speaker and may provide difficult compositional problems. In the case of Dr. Sawhill, he had three choices: to speak on one half of the subject, to deliver two speeches, or to attempt to blend the two parts into one speech.

Thank you for inviting me to speak with you this afternoon at the annual Middle Atlantic Placement Association conference. I am honored and delighted to be here, and also to see several New York University faces in the audience: George Dinas of our Graduate School of Business Administration, and Phil Jones of our Placement Office.

As you know, I have a special interest in our two-pronged subject today: energy and the job market.

In fact, when Mike Ippolito invited me last March, my primary concern was on formulating a national energy policy and helping move the United States toward energy independence.

But today, as president of New York University, I have a

special responsibility to train and guide young men and women as they begin their college careers and start to think about seeking jobs in the real world.

I see these two assignments as closely aligned. In the first instance, during my service in Washington, I tried to delineate the dimensions of the energy problem to the American people. In the second instance, I now have the opportunity of trying to help solve the problem I defined by providing skilled manpower to work in the field.

I would like to spend a few moments with you discussing those two concerns—America's energy independence and, its manpower needs. First I would like to share with you some of my observations on the serious nature of our energy problem, and suggest some ways to work ourselves out of it. And then I would like to show how, if the United States is to succeed in reasserting its independence, we will need to mobilize the resources of our population—and how you can help in that process.

Almost two years have passed since the Arab oil embargo began and the United States began developing an energy consciousness. Yet the nation is no closer today to a coherent, effective national energy policy than it was then.

Washington is in a stalemate. Most of what we hear from Congress and the Executive Branch are charges and counter-charges. Meanwhile, prices are going up, our dependence on imports is rising to 40 percent of our consumption, and thus our vulnerability to another embargo is greater than ever. I was glad to see that a temporary agreement has finally been reached in Washington on price controls.

We cannot let the OPEC cartel managers dictate American economic policy. At the same time, Americans must recognize that the days of low-cost, abundant energy are over —prices must be permitted to gradually increase to stimulate additional production and discourage unnecessary consumption.

Clearly we are in a precarious and intolerable position.

Even as we sit here today, the oil ministers have been sitting in Vienna and deciding to charge an additional 10 percent for their product.

So this is a good time for us to take stock—to see where we are and how we should proceed.

I think it is important to begin by discussing a major structural change that has taken place in the international oil industry in recent years. That change involves a shift in power from the giant international oil companies to governments of producer countries. Where once the oil giants controlled oil prices and the oil distribution system, today the control is in the hands of the major producing countries —Iran, Saudi Arabia, Venezuela, Kuwait, Nigeria, etc. The companies have lost the bargaining position they once had and are now forced to accept terms dictated by producer governments. As a result, a vacuum has been created, and the governments of the consuming countries are moving, of necessity, to fill this vacuum by entering into negotiations for oil supplies.

Much talk has taken place in Washington on the question of how to get the government more involved in international oil and in the financing of energy-resource development. Earlier this year, the House considered and rejected a proposal to create a Federal Petroleum Purchasing Agency, and Senator Frank Church of Idaho introduced legislation calling for an Oil Import Administration. The intent of both bills was to put the United States government into a better position to negotiate oil prices and supplies with the producing nations. While it is unlikely that Congress will take any action on this matter in 1975, it is clear that government-industry relationships are about to change. The cost and availability of energy are too affected with public interest to be left in the hands of an international cartel (OPEC) and an oil industry which no longer commands an effective position at the bargaining table.

President Ford last week suggested an Energy Indepen-

dence Authority that would have the power to distribute up to $100 billion in seed money in order to achieve energy self-sufficiency.

I have some important differences with the President over his plan. I am concerned, first, that this new agency would not be subject to congressional review, or to Civil Service hiring procedures. Second, there is not one word in the plan about energy conservation, which certainly must be the keystone of any energy master plan that we adopt. Third, the plan envisions a major new intrusion of the government into the private sector—a startling proposal from a President who spends his weekends traveling around the countryside talking about how he is going to get the government out of our hair. And finally, perhaps ironically, as the New York *Times* has pointed out, the plan the President outlined for the energy industry is the same type of plan that he is denying to cities and states seeking federal assistance.

Certainly, this debate over the appropriate role for the federal government will continue. At this point no one really knows how the public interest can best be served. In the meantime, however, the financial pressures of higher oil prices continue to mount.

Consider for a moment the impact of the sharp increases in prices which we have experienced over the past two years. According to the London-based journal, *The Economist,* the *surplus* money of the members of the Organization of Petroleum Exporting Countries—what's left *after* they have paid for imports and domestic development—is running at about $60 billion a year . . . or $7 million an hour . . . or . . . $115,000 a second.

You can almost hear the time-bomb ticking. But listen a bit closer.

Eight hours of this surplus OPEC cash can buy one Lockheed C-5A. Ten days' worth can buy the Bank of America; seventy-nine days, the Exxon Corporation; 143 days, IBM; 1.8 years, all America's direct investments outside the United States; and 9.5 years of surplus OPEC cash can buy all of the

stocks of all of the companies listed on the New York Stock Exchange.

From these figures it is clear that the situation is serious and will continue to worsen. Unless we take action soon, there will be less for payrolls in America and more for bankers in Baghdad.

The governments of the consuming nations must come to grips with the financial difficulties involved in the present flood of Western cash into the deserts of the Middle East. Reducing the deficits of the consuming nations and the surpluses of the producers—in short, avoiding international financial chaos—will require a sustained and concerted effort by the industrialized Free World. And this country—not only because it still remains the economic and moral leader of the Free World, but also because it has been the world's most profligate consumer of energy—must lead the way.

Now, some have suggested that the simple answer to the energy crisis is to increase production and find substitutes for scarce commodities. And, I would agree that we must develop our own abundant domestic energy resources: coal, natural gas and oil, and we must prepare for the transition to the next generation of resources—fusion and solar energy.

But that solution, by itself, sounds and in fact is, too simple.

It takes up to three years to develop an oil field after it's found, four or five years to open a new deep coal mine, five years to build a new refinery—perhaps eight with local resistance—and eight to ten years to construct a nuclear generating plant. And time-lags are just one of the obstacles on the road to self-sufficiency.

We will, of course, need to develop oil fields, open coal mines, build refineries and synthetic fuels plants, and nuclear power plants. The capital requirements for these activities will be staggering. But the other and equally enormous problem concerns manpower, about which I will say more in a few moments.

However, apart from the economic problems associated

with a crash program for independence, the effort might well require unacceptable environmental sacrifices—sacrifices which future generations would pay for. And we must be mindful that for many Americans our environmental legacy to these future generations is every bit as precious to them as our legacy of economic growth.

We can well appreciate, for example, the sentiments of people in the Rocky Mountain area who fear that their region might become the Appalachia of the 1970s and 1980s.

For all these reasons, I concluded that the government had the responsibility of pacing the development of additional energy resources at levels that can be sustained by the rest of the economy, that can be justified in terms of environmental costs, and that minimize social disruption.

And that consideration brings me to the short-run imperative of national energy policy: for the immediate future, the single most effective—in fact, the only—option we have is energy conservation.

Now, some have said that reduced energy consumption means a stagnant economy, a lower gross national product and hence, a loss of national wealth and prominence. This is simply not true.

Five other Western countries have per capita incomes which approximate ours, yet their average per capita energy consumption is roughly half that of the United States.

It seems eminently clear to those who would study the facts that energy conservation—using less energy and using it more efficiently—need not jeopardize the economic strength of the nation.

Yet, as I said earlier, we stand today no closer to a solution to our energy problem than we did during the embargo. The obvious question, then, is "Why?" Why have we failed to discipline ourselves to drive smaller, more energy-efficient automobiles, to live and work in more energy-efficient buildings, to stimulate recycling of waste materials, and to adopt other programs which would make us a more energy-conscious nation?

The answer, I believe, reflects the political stagnation in Washington—an unelected President from a minority party, and an overwhelmingly Democratic yet discouragingly undisciplined and ineffectual Congress with inept and unimaginative leadership—and all of the players posturing for 1976.

Progress comes slowly in that politicized environment, with its many energy fiefdoms and self-styled energy czars. It is difficult sometimes to know who to compromise with—especially given the independent attitude of the freshmen and many committee chairmen.

But there are fundamental and deep divisions between the President and the Congress. Basically, the President believes that we can make major cuts in energy consumption by sharply increasing energy prices. The actions that he has proposed would force up prices across the whole spectrum of petroleum products and work their way through the entire economy. Industrial fuels, feedstocks for the plastics industries, competitive fuels, all would be affected. Most estimates of the "ripple" effect go as high as $30 to $50 billion in increased prices at the consumer level.

On the other hand, the various congressional plans generally emphasize a more gradual reduction in oil imports than the Ford proposals and a more moderate increase in energy taxes. In addition, they contain tougher energy conservation measures and are more oriented toward environmental concerns.

But despite its inability yet to formulate a comprehensive energy plan, I believe we will see some new legislation this year. Congress will probably take steps to open up the naval petroleum reserves to production, create strategic reserves (oil stockpiles), gradually deregulate and therefore increase the price of natural gas, and take some steps towards exploration of the outer continental shelf—perhaps under a greater than usual degree of federal government supervision. We will not, however, get another bill to regulate strip mining, amendments to the Clean Air Act to permit utilities

to switch from oil to coal or an energy facilities siting bill.

To reduce energy consumption, it now seems likely that Congress will approve the proposal of the House for a tax credit to home owners who insulate their homes and install storm windows, and provide subsidies to those people in lower-income groups who cannot take advantage of such a tax credit. At the same time, we will probably see legislation which requires that new buildings be constructed in a more energy-efficient manner—perhaps a requirement that states develop energy-oriented building codes which are subject to review by the federal government. Congress is also considering regulatory programs to require the production of more energy-efficient automobiles, although the powerful automobile lobby is fighting—with considerable success—attempts to make these regulations mandatory.

In the last analysis, Congress must sooner or later face up to the tough decision of reducing gasoline consumption and demonstrate to the rest of the world that the United States is dead serious about energy conservation. I believe that the only way that we, as a nation, can really come to grips with declining energy supplies, is to enact mandatory efficiency standards for automobiles and a moderate but gradually increasing gasoline tax—accompanied by refunds to those who would otherwise suffer undue hardships. These actions would bring about some savings immediately, and more importantly, they would signal a future of gradually higher prices for both gasoline and gas guzzlers. Based on this signal, consumers and auto manufacturers could plan and act accordingly. The transition to a more efficient auto fleet would be steady and rapid, and the revenues generated by the tax could be used to influence energy R & D, improve public transportation facilities and help reduce the growing federal deficit.

Unfortunately, with so much at stake in the next election, it is doubtful that we will see any significant progress towards reducing gasoline consumption until 1977. Congress,

I am afraid, has been letting short-run political considerations outweigh this important longer-range goal.

I would remind the Congress, however, of the high costs associated with continued inaction. Eighty-five percent of the proposed gasoline tax would have been refunded to the American people in the form of tax rebates and higher reductions. Not one cent of the OPEC price increases are similarly refunded. Thus, by failing to act responsibly to curb energy consumption, the Congress has created the conditions which enabled OPEC to raise their prices.

Now, having painted that somewhat bleak picture of the economic and political situation, let me turn to some of the longer-term problems of preparing our young people to deal with the energy-resource-development activities on which our nation will be embarking over the next few decades.

Employment in the energy sector is a relatively small portion of total employment—about 2 percent—yet the industry accounts for a large share of employment in certain occupations. For instance, it employs 76 percent of all petroleum engineers, 42 percent of all geologists, 21 percent of all mining engineers. And in general, those who work in energy-producing industries require more education and training than those in the general labor force.

Most of our concern today is with college-trained professionals in the energy industry—and that is where some critical shortages are forecast for the years ahead.

Nevertheless, we should not overlook the demands that will be placed upon the labor market. A very serious shortage of skilled tradesmen in the construction industry may well develop over the next three years. And this could mean a slow-down in our rate of energy production. It has happened already. For instance, of the 28 nuclear power plants scheduled to open in 1973, at least 5 were delayed because of an insufficient labor supply. And between now and 1978, the construction requirements will double for plumbers, pipefitters, welders, electricians, boilermakers, millwrights and carpenters.

Another example is in the coal industry, where by 1985 we will need an additional 170,000 miners if we are to meet that industry's goal of tripling coal production. Yet the population of coal miners today is declining.

And after the miners bring it out of the ground, we still need to learn what to do with coal. We will need scientists to tell us how best to utilize this most abundant natural resource—how to burn it cleanly, how to convert it to oil and gas. From the R & D standpoint in the coal industry alone, we will need a tenfold increase in the number of scientists and engineers.

And in the nuclear power industry, there will be great demand for engineers and technicians. To illustrate the problem, as recently as 1970 nuclear power provided only 1 percent of the energy used in this country—about as much as firewood. But by the end of this century, just twenty-five years from now, nuclear power will be expected to provide as much as 50 percent of our national energy needs.

We are concerned today with providing the "indirect" production personnel who can make that happen—the scientists, engineers and technicians.

The National Science Foundation completed a study in 1974 which indicated that a growth of certain occupations in the energy sector more rapid than that in the general economy could potentially limit our development of energy resources.

In particular, the design and construction of energy facilities will necessitate expansion of the professional and technical staffs of architectural and engineering firms, and the design branches of construction firms. The NFS study cited a substantial future shortage of mechanical engineers experienced in refinery design, and noted that requirements for such engineers are expected to double between 1974 and 1985. In addition, employment of engineers in the design of nuclear power plants is expected to double during the same period of time.

The petroleum industry today cannot hire enough

trained individuals to meet its expanding needs. Mechanical engineers are most in demand, according to an *Oil and Gas Journal* survey, followed by chemical engineers, civil engineers, petroleum and electrical engineers. Also listed among the hardest-to-find disciplines were geophysicists and geologists.

Similarly, more thousands of engineers will be needed to build a synthetic fuels industry—yet the nation's engineering class of 1976 will probably be the smallest in the last twenty years.

And this is ironic because, only a few years ago, guidance counselors were directing students away from careers in engineering because there were too many of them and many were unemployed.

So we do need to pace and plan for our manpower growth, and we do need some controls on manpower development. None of us wants to see again the situation that engineers found themselves in a few years ago when the aerospace industry began declining.

Just eleven days ago, the first freshman class of my tenure as president entered their classrooms. These young men and women joined 8.6 million other collegians enrolled across the country this fall.

It is appropriate that we ask ourselves, as educators and as businessmen, what they will find when they graduate. Certainly this means keeping a watchful eye on short-term and long-term manpower needs in a wide spectrum of fields. The changeability of these needs means that we need to ask ourselves frequently whether today's college students will be equipped with the business skills and the basic tools required to meet the demands of new careers, new kinds of work, in a constantly changing market place.

And, importantly, whether they will also have the literary, artistic and social skills required to function in modern society. It is vital that we provide students with essential guidance so they will be able to make sound judgments when planning their careers.

Recent developments in the employment market should reinforce our dedication to the concept of career planning. Between 1969 and 1975, the job market for college graduates has shifted dramatically and starting salaries for male college graduates have dropped sharply.

Consequently, there has been a marked decline in the proportion of young men choosing to enroll in college. Between 1969 and 1974, the proportion of eighteen-to-nineteen-year-old men enrolled in college fell from 44 percent to 33 percent, and the percentage of young women leveled off.

Whether this is a relatively short run cyclical occurrence or a long-term trend is still open to question. But, at least for the immediate future, the message is clear: we must redouble our efforts to assist our graduates in obtaining employment, and we must ensure that our programs prepare students for careers.

Regardless of a student's chosen field of study, our goal must always be to educate people in the fundamentals of communication, analysis and problem solving. Curriculums should combine a rich background in liberal education with more specialized training in a specific area. An example of this training are the applied science programs, which offer an interdisciplinary education to assure that those with specialties in scientific or technical fields gain a working appreciation of the economic, corporate and societal factors which influence the functioning of all large-scale service systems. I believe such combined degree programs will more than prove their worth in the years ahead. At New York University we currently have eighteen combined degree programs which facilitate career planning. At our School of Law, for example, a student can wed his JD training with a Master in Urban Planning, a Master of Public Administration, or a Master in Business Administration.

The legal thicket of the energy-environment jungle will only be penetrable by corporate planners, government administrators and lawyers if they have the breadth of knowl-

edge to deal with the people and the disciplines involved.

In the future we will need to develop interdisciplinary research projects to solve some of the great problems we shall face in the last quarter of this century.

Consider, for instance, the skills that will be required to build a nuclear generating plant. A company will need a whole range of professionals: capital formation analysts; lawyers and architects with business degrees familiar with federal, state and local construction standards; local zoning lawyers conversant with nuclear technology; environmental/economic impact officials; sociological and ecological experts; architects and scientists with an understanding of the social and environmental implications of their actions. We will require a whole new population of energy businessmen: accountants, consumer experts, marketing specialists, and so on.

It is clear that the era of the lonely specialist is behind us. We are talking about the integration of professional skills into a complex energy system.

So the opportunities for those who enter the energy job market now are both diversified and fascinating. Such persons will participate in one of the most exciting, important and long-range projects in the history of the United States.

We are not just talking about a one-shot, boom-and-bust phenomenon. This is not another Manhattan project, or another race to put a man on the moon; nor is it like the crash development that accompanies wartime.

The business of energy cuts across so much territory that it will continue to provide opportunities for employment in numerous disciplines both within and outside the scientific and research fields for many years.

When I was at the Federal Energy Administration, we made a study on how to plan for orderly manpower development and how to avert prospective shortages.

Several specific actions were suggested. For instance, the federal government could take responsibility for providing a constant flow of timely and accurate information on the

occupations that will be needed in the energy sector, and where they will be needed.

We also discussed having the government work directly with universities to assist in their planning of training programs, methods of publicizing jobs, and ways to encourage placement.

Another thought was to establish a federal clearinghouse for energy-related jobs, that would identify current or potential skill shortages in the energy fields and make available to employers lists of candidates for hard-to-fill jobs.

And we suggested that the federal government, working through the educational system, could increase or establish scholarship assistance for selected curriculums. Educational grants could be provided to encourage the expansion of degree and nondegree programs in fields involving advanced skills and knowledge, particularly in geothermal, solar and nuclear energy technologies.

At New York University we stand ready to assist in this great national project. We will continue to prod the federal and state governments for support for higher education. And as a private institution, we believe that we offer a unique and considerable flexibility to select new disciplines, combine fields and study, and draw forth the best from our students. We shall continue to do our best to provide the type of talent that business and industry will need in the years ahead.

Thank you.

# TERRORISM, THE ULTIMATE EVIL [5]

## CLARENCE M. KELLEY [6]

During the past year the newspapers have been full of the Patty Hearst trial, the bombing in a New York airport, senseless murders of innocent bystanders in Boston, and racial anarchy in metropolitan areas. The *FBI Police Bulletin* (v 4 no 1) reported 89 bombings in 1975 attributed to terrorist activities as compared to 45 in 1974, and 24 in 1973. Since 1947 crime has increased in every year except 1972, when it dropped slightly. It was up 13 percent during the first half of 1975 (*U.S. News & World Report*, November 24, 1975).

In attempting to carry out its crime-fighting tasks, the FBI has had problems with its own image and methods, as has the CIA in its sphere. The US Senate Select Committee on Intelligence Activities under the chairmanship of Frank Church, Democratic Senator from Idaho, has investigated their activities, and many reports of alleged unethical practices have been leaked to the newspapers. The average citizen may be confused as to what the answer is to lawlessness.

On January 13, 1976, Clarence M. Kelley, director of the Federal Bureau of Investigation, responded to attacks on his agency in a speech entitled, "Terrorism, the Ultimate Evil," before a press luncheon of the American Security Council. The speech was an answer to the sensational exposés of the Senate Select Committee. When he read Director Kelley's speech into the *Congressional Record*, Samuel L. Devine, Republican Representative from Ohio, who earlier in his career (1940-1945) had served as a special agent for the FBI, explained Mr. Kelley's motivation in speaking:

> The American people have been spoon fed a distorted rehash of old allegations against the FBI by the select committees and a large segment of the press. . . .
>
> Staff members of the Senate Select Committee, speaking in tandem before television cameras and large numbers of press representatives taking hurried notes, on November 18, 1975, ticked off charge after charge against the FBI. Their comments were laced throughout with phrases and adjec-

[5] Delivered at the American Security Council Press luncheon, Washington, D.C., January 13, 1976. Quoted by permisson.
[6] For biographical note, see Appendix.

tives designed to influence conclusions based on emotion. . . .

They strongly condemned FBI actions in one case while declining to reveal information available which led to the actions. Their charges and conclusions led to big headlines in newspapers all across the country and occupied considerable time on the television and radio newscasts. . . .

It is time for the Congress and the press to stop kicking the FBI around for its few prior mistakes. This serves only to generate headlines and to further undermine the public trust and confidence in one of our most vital agencies. (*Congressional Record,* January 20, 1976).

Director Kelley, a career law enforcement officer who served in the FBI (1940-1961) and as chief of police in Kansas City, Missouri (1961-1973), took a hard line against violence. In his speech he devoted a major portion of his time to presenting the problems and less than two hundred words to the solution. He made an urgent plea to the public to help the law enforcement officers overcome lawlessness.

An answer to the charges against the FBI, the speech should also be considered a significant statement about crime and violence in this country.

As we Americans prepare to celebrate the two hundredth anniversary of our independence, I find myself increasingly concerned about the growing problem of terrorism.

It is a strange anomaly that we, the citizens of the freest major nation on earth, should find it necessary to concern ourselves with terrorism.

Yet we *must*—and that is the message I bring to you today. All Americans who cherish freedom, all Americans who would preserve orderly government and domestic tranquillity, must involve themselves in the effort to prevent terrorism from becoming a crisis problem in our society.

Some may say our concern *should* be directed toward failures in our society that spawn terrorism.

I disagree.

History is replete with instances where reforms did nothing to dissuade truly committed terrorists.

Alexander II of Russia in the 1860s emancipated the peasants and instituted land and other reforms beneficial to

the poor and oppressed. By our standards those measures were not spectacular; but back then they represented genuine social progress. Yet the response of the revolutionaries, frustrated in their efforts to whip up popular support, was to intensify their campaign of bombing and assassination.

And Alexander II himself eventually was murdered by revolutionaries.

To achieve tranquillity and order by appeasing avowed terrorists is not only unworkable, it's unthinkable.

Their rationale is too mercurial, inconsistent and twisted.

How do you reason with an individual who considers the murder and multilation of children an acceptable means to impose his will on others?

You don't.

The terrorist neither listens to reason nor engages in reasoning with others. His aim is to generate fear—to frighten people into submission.

He measures success by the magnitude of the fear he generates through brutal, savage acts of violence.

How proud those responsible must have been of the bombing at Fraunces Tavern in New York City last year—a bombing in which four persons were killed and scores were injured. Members of the Armed Forces of Puerto Rican Liberation crowed that they committed that vicious act and others.

Terrorists like these are prepared to kill men, women and children to further whatever cause they claim to be pursuing. And the heinousness of these murders is accented by the fact that they murder without passion. They murder with cool deliberation and careful planning.

Because they have no compunction whatsoever about killing human beings, they have no compunction about committing other crimes. They steal. They rob. They kidnap. They take hostages. They extort.

There are no depths to which they will not go to further their "cause."

Make no mistake about it, the true terrorist is *committed*—committed to an extent that is difficult for rational people to comprehend. A perverted sort of courage and profound dedication sustains them. They are humorless, insensitive and they are influenced by no truths other than those they perceive to validate their cause.

They are utterly amoral.

I have been in law enforcement thirty-five years. I have met and talked with murderers—murderers who have taken lives cruelly and viciously; but nevertheless, most of them have moments of compassion and gentleness.

The terrorist does not.

The law makes allowances for homicides that are committed without premeditation. The penalties are less severe. The law recognizes that there is an added evil in a murder that is planned and deliberate, with malice aforethought. And the penalties for such acts are more severe.

There is a dispassionate, impersonal cruelty in terroristic murders that adds an extra dimension of horror.

The terrorist's exploding bomb kills and maims indiscriminately—the young, the elderly, the robust, the infirm —people who have absolutely no inkling of the terrorist's perceived grievance or cause.

As far as I'm concerned, terrorism is, indeed, the ultimate evil in our society. And no one can consider himself immune from terroristic acts.

I've met a couple of terrorists. One of them was planning to bomb my home in Kansas City before his arrest. He admitted it. Take my word for it, nothing can bring the evil of terrorism in perspective more quickly for a person than to learn he is a target.

I wonder how the American people view the revolutionary terrorist.

I fear many people see them as a caricatured comical figure, a bearded, rumpled individual furtively clutching a round bomb with fuse sputtering. It would be folly to confuse this invention of some cartoonist's mind with the true

revolutionary terrorist. He is not amusing. He is lethal. And Americans simply must realize this.

And Americans should be aware there has been strong evidence in the past couple of years that our terrorist problem is growing.

There were 89 bombings attributable to terrorist activity in our nation last year, as compared to 45 in 1974 and 24 in 1973.

During the past five years there have been 255 such bombings, 122 firebombings, 45 sniping incidents, 120 shootings, 24 ambushes and 21 arsons.

Eleven persons were killed in terrorist acts of violence in 1975. And 72 people were injured. Property damage amounted to more than $2.7 million.

I don't know how well statistics can convey the true extent of the terrorist menace; but one figure that is particularly revealing to me is the number of police officers attacked.

Since 1971, the deaths of at least 43 officers and the wounding of 152 more have been linked to terrorists.

Sometimes one terrorist group or another writes a letter to the news media boasting of successful ambush attacks on law enforcement officers.

Still, I think to most Americans, the terrorist threat is a remote and abstract thing—a problem that commands little, if any, of their attention in their understandable preoccupation with problems more immediate in the everyday business of living.

They may review with revulsion news reports of terrorist activities around the globe—the bloody atrocities in Northern Ireland, the Middle East, and elsewhere.

They may be momentarily dismayed by occasional news reports of such activity in the United States. But thus far this activity has been scattered across our nation; and the total impact of this activity is not easily perceived by the public.

But the families of those killed and maimed have per-

ceived it. Nothing I could say, no figures I could cite, could speak more articulately of the terrorists' menace than the cold, still and mutilated bodies of their victims.

All right. Granted we have a growing terrorist problem, what is the FBI doing about it?

Everything we possibly can within the parameters of law.

The importance of our intelligence work in this area cannot be overstated. In our intelligence work we have striven—and have succeeded in many instances—to prevent bloodshed and property loss.

Unfortunately our successes are rarely publicized, nor is it possible to make public some of them; to do so could jeopardize the safety of innocent persons who helped us.

We also have worked arduously to bring to justice those who commit such acts. It is not an easy endeavor. And we have been criticized for taking so long to apprehend alleged terrorists who are fugitives.

But it should be recognized that we are dealing for the most part with small, closely knit, clandestine groups difficult to penetrate. Some have achieved expertise in preparing false identifications. And they are able to lose themselves in a subculture of communes that spans the United States.

Incredibly, some otherwise law-abiding people provide moral and material support to terrorists, apparently for idealistic reasons. The best that can be said about such people is that they are terribly misguided.

Terrorists are not idealists. They are without principle. They have no regard for human life. They pervert the freedoms this nation bestows upon its citizens. They defile American traditions. They are not political activists. They are criminals. And their numbers seem to be growing.

I'm not saying that our nation is in imminent danger of being devastated by terrorists. But I *do* consider terrorism a very *real and growing problem.*

And I think it's vital that Americans involve themselves in the effort to stem terrorist acts *before* they reach crisis intensity.

How can citizens combat terrorism?

First, by recognizing the true, despicable nature of the terrorist.

By supporting law enforcement in its efforts to frustrate these peddlers of death and destruction.

By promptly reporting information pertaining to terrorism.

By vigorously supporting the principle of rule by laws that has enabled our nation to flourish these two hundred years.

We are a nation of about 214 million people—heterogeneous, industrious, robust and peace-loving. No two of us are exactly alike. We usually differ, sometimes vehemently, on major issues and national priorities.

But we have at least one thing in common.

*We cherish freedom.* We are unified in that. And let those terrorists who boast that they will bring the fireworks to our Bicentennial celebration take note of this: Americans will not permit themselves to be divested of that freedom.

Let the terrorists know that their mindless acts of violence can only strengthen Americans' resolve to preserve our democratic system that has served us so well these two centuries.

Thank you.

# ON THE CAMPAIGN TRAIL

## REDISCOVERING AMERICA [1]

### FRANK CHURCH [2]

At 10:00 A.M. on October 20, 1975, Frank Church, senior Senator (Democrat) from Idaho, addressed the opening session of the California League of Cities, assembled in the Grand Ballroom of the Hilton Hotel, San Francisco. He was introduced by Lee Davies, mayor of Modesto, California. He spoke to an audience of about 3,400 composed of mayors, councilmen, police chiefs, fire chiefs, other city officials, and interested citizens.

Frank Church is one of the most eloquent US senators. Since the time at age sixteen when he won the national American Legion oratorical contest, he has prided himself on speaking effectively before diverse audiences. One source has described him as follows:

> In person he is trim, ebullient, tall (six feet) with a tan face that grins easily, brown eyes, Indian black hair with some features of gray in it, and a warmth that the camera somehow doesn't catch. The one constant, on camera or off, is the voice, a soft baritone that falls in measured cadences like lines from Tennyson . . . (Christopher Lyon, New York *Times,* June 15, 1975).

Consistent with what William E. Borah, another great Idaho senator and a most vocal isolationist, might have said forty years ago, Church gave his speech an isolationist flavor. Saying that the time had come to stop attempting to solve the problems of other nations and to stop financing space exploration, he argued from the thesis "We must bring the federal focus home again" (meaning focus upon city problems)—hence his title, "Rediscovering America." The structure of the speech was simple. After a clever *introduction,* built around the story concerning his father-in-law, he devoted a major portion of his remarks to the *problem:* The focus of the federal government, dissipated by corruption and unwise procedures, has mistakenly been upon foreign problems

[1] Delivered to the annual meeting of the membership of the California League of Cities, Hilton Hotel, San Francisco, October 20, 1975. Quoted by permission.
[2] For biographical note, see Appendix.

and space problems. His *solution* was that the federal government must play "a more helpful role" in contributing to the well-being of the cities. In his brief *conclusion* he pleaded for energetic "community" involvement. Church was highly effective before city officials beset with unemployment, physical deterioration, racial antagonisms, striking municipal employees, and unbalanced budgets.

This speech is not one of Church's major efforts, but it stirs the emotions of his listeners. (For a more eloquent speech by Church, see the one delivered to a college audience in 1970, REPRESENTATIVE AMERICAN SPEECHES, 1970-1971, p 49-62.)

For many years until his death, my chief political adviser, critic, cheerleader, and friend was my father-in-law, Chase Clark. He was then a federal judge, but he had held many elective offices. He had served in both houses of the state Legislature; he had been governor of Idaho and mayor of Idaho Falls. The hardest job of all, he used to say, was being mayor of Idaho Falls.

Yet that was the job which brought him the most satisfaction. People were constantly after him, phoning him at all hours, day and night.

"Mayor, the leaves from my neighbor's tree are blowing all over my front yard!"

"Well, Ma'am, what do you expect me to do, come catch them in my hat?"

The pressure never let up. Even on the golf course they pursued him from green to green. Still, he loved his work because he was so close to the people and they were so close to him.

The new library he built, the landscaping along the river banks he started, the municipal golf course he opened, not only mattered at the time, but have contributed to a better life in Idaho Falls ever since.

It is often said that people care most about their city governments because city governments are the nearest to them. But there is another, more telling reason:

City governments are relevant. Everyone in a city feels keenly the quality of police or fire protection, of traffic con-

trol, of garbage removal and sewage treatment. Parks, zoos, and playgrounds bring joy to our children. Municipal hospitals are truly a life and death matter.

City government renders services that we can see and feel, services that make sense.

Some cities may perform these services badly; others may perform them well. Either way, the people are not indifferent to local government. They are intensely interested, because the decisions made at City Hall affect their lives in direct, tangible and vital ways.

In short, city government hits us where we live—quite literally.

But the federal government is quite a different matter. Its seat in Washington is far removed from the people at large. It seems remote. And people often feel that they are powerless to do much about its decisions. Because of that, the national government is handicapped.

Being number two in the hearts of the people, it has had to try harder. Americans have felt friendly toward the federal government during periods when it was presided over by Presidents they could respect, and when it was coping with problems close to home.

During the Great Depression of the thirties—a national calamity beyond the reach of state and local governments—it was Franklin Roosevelt who loomed so large. Federal relief programs put men and women back to work; federal guarantees enabled them to obtain the loans with which to buy homes; federal insurance reopened the nation's banks; the national government was at work mending the tattered economy in every home town, restoring hope and prosperity to the lives of the people.

It was the federal government that produced Social Security and, later, Medicare with which to ease the evening of our lives.

It was the federal government that called a halt to racial segregation and demanded equal justice in every corner of our land for citizens of every color and kind.

Perhaps nothing as massive, distant and faceless as the federal government can ever be loved. But when that government functioned in the realm of the relevant, it earned the respect of the people. When that government was lawful and clean, it was neither loathed nor feared.

But, oh, how that has changed. The respect has been shattered. The trust has been lost. The friendly relationship between the government and the people has been severely strained.

And no wonder!

Our former President, the one human face the national government wears, proved unfaithful to his duty and untruthful to his countrymen. He was run out of office a step ahead of impeachment.

His chosen vice president preceded him, resigning office within the shadow of the criminal court where he had copped a plea to a twenty-two-count criminal indictment!

But the lawlessness goes deeper. It reaches into the federal agencies on which we have customarily relied to adhere to the law . . . the FBI, the CIA, the Internal Revenue Service, and even the Post Office Department.

Our intelligence service hires the Mafia to make a hit on a foreign leader; it dispenses poisons to dispose of troublesome politicians abroad; and it flaunts the law to spy on American citizens in our own land.

For twenty years our private mail is secretly opened and photographed.

Churches, charities, educational foundations, universities, newspapers and magazines, along with civil rights leaders, actors, mayors, columnists and elected officials are placed on "watch lists" for purposes of surveillance.

The IRS, at the request of other federal agencies, opens tax investigations against citizens who are not suspected of tax delinquency. Last year, nearly thirty thousand income tax returns were turned over to the federal agencies having nothing to do with tax collection, but which sought the information for purposes of their own.

The FBI sets up an elaborate program to harass, discredit and endanger law-abiding citizens whose only offense is that of opposing government policies, which our laws and Constitution guarantee them the right to do.

Justice Louis Brandeis once wrote:

Decency, security and liberty alike demand that government officials shall be subjected to the same rules of conduct that are commands to the citizens. In a government of laws, existence of the government shall be imperiled, if it fails to observe the law scrupulously. Our government is the potent, the omnipresent teacher. For good or ill, it teaches the whole people by its example.

What a wise and prophetic statement! For the federal government, in recent years, has not only misled the people by its bad example, it has been the main victim of its own malpractices. It has brought itself into disrepute.

All this can—and must—be corrected. The investigation of wrongdoing within the government which I presently chair is exposing the unlawful conduct of the CIA, the FBI, and other federal agencies. But we shall also propose reforms that can restore public confidence in these agencies and return them to the prestigious position they should enjoy in our society.

We need the FBI. We need the CIA. But ours is a government of law. We must see to it that these agencies conduct themselves in the future strictly within the law!

That will help.

But it is just a start.

Once federal agencies begin to set a good example again, by administering their affairs in proper and lawful ways, I suggest that the policy makers on the banks of the Potomac should celebrate 1976, our Bicentennial year, by rediscovering America!

The federal government was established in the first place, not to remake the world, but to promote the welfare of the people of the United States. For too long have our Presidents lost themselves in dubious foreign pursuits. The

delusion that we could act as the world's policeman, banker and judge, has distorted federal spending beyond belief—and lead us far afield. Consider, if you will, the following examples:

1. Our peacetime military budget now exceeds the level of military spending during any previous war. Costs have become irrational. We are spending $1.5 billion to build a single submarine. That's a thousand times as much as a submarine cost in World War II. We are planning to build a fleet of bombers for $100 million apiece. Nobody can explain how the bombers could add to our defense anything approaching their cost. Such extravagance in the skies above soaks up the money we need so badly here below.

2. Foreign aid has assumed a life of its own. Despite unemployment in the United States that is way above that of any other industrialized country, we continue to dole out about $10 billion a year to foreign governments. And the price tag is going up instead of going down!

3. Having demonstrated several times over our ability to land an American on the moon, we pump new billions into space to catch a closer glimpse of dead planets.

I submit to you, that even if the American people liked the government in Washington, they couldn't make sense of it. Why should our own cities be of less concern to the federal government than the preservation of some faltering foreign principality? If, during the past demented decade, the federal government had spent a tenth as much salvaging our own biggest city as it squandered on Saigon, New York would not be teetering on the brink of bankruptcy today.

We must bring the federal focus home again. If it is our peculiar passion to make everything right in the world, where better to begin than in our own disordered house? If the President must counsel with important leaders, let him start with the mayors. Who else lives as close to the heartbeat of the people?

I wish I had a platter full of panaceas for our cities. But,

as you know so well, nobody holds such a platter. There are no quick fixes. Of course, nothing would help so much as an economic recovery that would end this recession. Still, restoring our cities to robust health will be a long, painstaking process. The slide down is swift compared with the climb back.

But the federal government, I should think, could play a more helpful role. Until prosperity returns to fill the municipal coffers again, other American cities besides New York will soon find themselves in desperate straits. And many a state government will follow close behind. Illinois has already run out of money and must borrow against next year's revenues if state funds are to continue to flow to its cities.

The dilemma is captured in a single statistic gleaned from a study by the Congressional Research Service: Out of 140 local governments surveyed, 122 entered the current fiscal year with a combined surplus of $340 million and will end the year with a $40 million deficit.

Where getting over the hump means floating municipal bonds, a federal guarantee could be of great assistance in marketing the bonds and tempering the interest rate. For years, the federal government has done as much for the big corporations. A federal agency called the Overseas Private Investment Corporation, OPIC for short, furnishes insurance, not available on the private market, to American companies wishing to invest abroad. The insurance, heavily subsidized by the taxpayers, protects the foreign investments of these companies against war risks or confiscation or the inconvertibility of the foreign currency.

OPIC is just another example of the federal government's preoccupation with the foreign scene. These big companies are busily exporting American jobs. I say we should stop underwriting the calculated risks of multinational corporations which don't go broke, and start standing behind our own weakened cities which do!

It would also help immensely if the federal government

would start eliminating the bureaucratic maze which so complicates its efforts to assist the cities. When President Eisenhower left office, there were some 100 federal grant-in-aid programs costing $7 billion annually. When President Johnson departed, there were 530, costing $24 billion. Now there are 975, costing $52 billion annually. The Department of Health, Education, and Welfare alone has 274 such programs, each administered by its own bureaucracy, each requiring comparable bureaucracies at state and local levels to apply for and administer the grants.

The smaller cities of Idaho that I represent can't cope with the administrative cost of deciphering these myriad programs, let alone applying and qualifying for their aid. Even those cities that are large enough to hire such specialists are adding to their overhead, wasting money that could be better spent on direct services to their citizens.

Perhaps the best way to cut the Gordian knot is to move from specific, strings-attached, Washington-administered grants-in-aid programs toward more general bloc revenue sharing. That would accomplish two goals: (1) It would give the cities the flexibility to buy what they need, rather than what Washington decides they need; and (2) it would trim back administrative expenses at both ends.

Finally, in the longer term, we must anticipate and prepare for a reversal of the middle-class flight from the central cities. The coming age of high-priced fuel is already making the short commute more appealing.

But a major obstacle to the return of the lemmings from the suburban seas—and along with them their properties and higher taxable incomes—is the decay of the housing they abandoned. But these neighborhoods will never be revived if we have to wait for HUD to do it.

A new way must be found, which looks not to Washington, but to the city governments, instead. Relying on community leaders to find solutions suited to the local need, rather than depending on the abstractions of federal planners, typifies what I believe must be the new approach.

In my state, agricultural researchers consult constantly, in the field, with Idaho farmers, both to find out what new soil and crop problems are appearing, and to learn if earlier laboratory experiments are working. The theory is that farmers know a whole lot about farming.

At the risk of seeming parochial, I suggest that the people who know most about city problems—and how we might best go about solving them—are the people who manage the cities.

God willing, let us find the wisdom to turn to the mayors and the city managers in our search for solutions.

# PRESIDENTIAL REMARKS
## WITH QUESTION-AND-ANSWER SESSION [3]

### GERALD R. FORD [4]

The presidential primaries are a kind of quadrennial binge that exhausts the contenders, wearies the voters, confuses the issues, and costs millions of dollars. In spite of these drawbacks, almost any politician who hopes for the presidency must join the competition. Not taking his nomination for granted, President Gerald Ford seems to have been campaigning since he became President. According to one source, he has assembled "the largest and most sophisticated public relations apparatus that has ever existed in the White House." He has at least eight speech writers and many advisers (John Herbers, New York *Times*, June 18, 1975).

When Ronald Reagan made his appearance, Ford and his helpers stepped up their efforts. But not until the North Carolina primary (March 23, 1976), after Ford had won five states, was Reagan able to top the President. Contrasting the two Republicans, R. W. Apple Jr. of the New York *Times* (November 21, 1975) described the Californian as "a vivid campaigner, a trained performer who works effortless turns of humor, modesty, outrage and concern upon his audiences." He thought that Ford was "a plodder on the stump, unexciting and sometimes bumbling." Another reporter changed the description slightly, saying that Ford was "nice but bumbling, friendly but indecisive, the kind of man who would make a good neighbor, but who lacks the leadership to be a good President" (Dennis Farney, *Wall Street Journal*, January 14, 1976).

Ford's stumping in Illinois, March 5 and 6, 1976, was a good example of the demands that campaigning made upon a presidential hopeful. During the previous week in Florida, where he won, he made nineteen appearances, always with a brief speech and questions (*Presidential Documents*, March 8, 1976).

On March 5 and 6, he spent two strenuous days in Illinois where "generally large, enthusiastic crowds greeted . . . [him] at

---

[3] Delivered at Bradley University's Everett McKinley Dirksen Forum, Robertson Memorial Fieldhouse, Peoria, Illinois, at 8:20 P.M. March 5, 1976. Material taken from *Weekly Compilation of Presidential Documents*, March 15, 1976, vol. 12, no. 11.

[4] For biographical note, see Appendix.

almost every stop" (Washington *Post,* March 7, 1976). His appearances on March 5 showed how tightly Ford was scheduled:

> 12:10 P.M. Remarks at the unveiling of cornerstone for the
> Lincoln Home, National Visitors' Center, Springfield,
> Illinois
> 2:05 P.M. Remarks and question-and-answer session at a
> farm forum, Springfield
> 3:10 P.M. Remarks to a group of Illinois teachers of children
> with impaired hearing, Springfield
> 3:45 P.M. Remarks at committee reception, Springfield
> 5:45 P.M. Remarks to reporters upon arrival at the Greater
> Peoria Airport, Peoria, Illinois
> 8:20 P.M. Remarks and question-and-answer session, Bradley
> University, Everett McKinley Dirksen Forum, at Robert-
> son Memorial Fieldhouse, Peoria
> 9:10 P.M. Remarks to members of Shrine, Mohammed Tem-
> ple, Peoria

The following day, March 6, between 9:10 A.M. and 6:05 P.M.,
he made six additional appearances in three other Illinois cities
(*Presidential Documents,* March 12, 1976) before returning to
Washington.

On March 5, 1976, after a strenuous day of appearances, Ford
spoke to an audience of 7,200 at Bradley University's Everett Mc-
Kinley Dirksen Forum. Intending this speech as an answer to Reagan, Ford turned his attention to foreign policy and defense. The
Washington *Post* (March 7, 1976) reported that "the speech was
notable because for the first time in the campaign the President
spoke openly about the threat of nuclear war." John Osborne
thought that this speech was "his best public performance since he
succeeded Richard Nixon. The audience was friendly, alert, responsive. Mr. Ford dealt briskly and knowledgeably with questions" (*New Republic,* April 10, 1976, p 8-9).

The speech was probably largely prepared by Ford's speech
writers. The thirteen appearances within two days required the
assembling of extensive notes to enable the President to include
all of the necessary local references. In the Bradley University
speech the President spent almost half of his prepared "remarks"
flattering the natives, referring to basketball star Chet Walker,
Representative Bob Michel, Mayor Richard E. Carver, Bradley
University and, of course, "Ev" Dirksen. It is difficult to judge
whether the questions were spontaneous or planted. Ford's staff
may have prepared the questions and appointed party faithfuls to
present them. In answering at least one question the President did

not have all his facts straight. He expressed disgust that the Air Force decided to withdraw the AFR Officers Training Corps, saying "we will do our darnedest to rectify the error." The facts were that Bradley had fallen below the required minimum number of ROTC entrants (*New Republic,* April 10, 1976, p 95).

In spite of caricatures by comedians and depreciating remarks of commentators, Ford continues to project the image of a plain and open man with a common touch. He takes Harry Truman as a model and strives not for eloquence but for credibility. As the intensity of the campaign builds, he seems to improve his platform effectiveness and is at his best responding to questions.

At the outset, let me say I don't think we would have scheduled this tonight if I had known that Chet Walker was being honored last night. [*Laughter*] I probably would have been here last night if I could have, because I am a great fan of his, and I am a great fan of all that Bradley University stands for in the field of basketball, as well as academic standing, and I congratulate you. And I'm darn glad and lucky to be the recipient of the Everett McKinley Dirksen Honorary Chair here tonight. I thank you very, very much.

Bob Michel was much too generous and far too kind, but it's nice to hear in 1976. And I thank Bob for not only his kind words, but his long friendship. And I could reciprocate in kind for the outstanding job that he does for all of you in the Congress of the United States.

Obviously, it's a great pleasure and privilege and a very high honor for me to be here tonight, not only in Bradley but in the city of Peoria. And I thank Mayor Carver for his warm and very kind reception at the airport.

I have been here—yes, back in 1949, but I have been here subsequent to that, and I am impressed with your people, your administration, and the objectives and the kind of morale that you have here in Peoria. You set a high standard for other communities around the country.

The trustees of this University have been very kind and honored me in a very personal way with an honorary appointment to the Everett McKinley Dirksen Chair of Gov-

ernment and Public Affairs. And I am deeply honored,
because Everett Dirksen was one of the finest public servants
I have ever known, and history will record him as one of the
most gifted and beloved men ever to serve in the Congress
of the United States.

Ev and I became especially close during the years when
he served as the Republican leader in the United States
Senate and I was his counterpart in the House of Representatives. Ev Dirksen was more than a statesman, more
than a master of legislative process, more than a never-to-
be-forgotten speaker. I knew him as a good friend, a wise
counselor, and an inspiring teacher.

He taught us one of his most unforgettable lessons on
the memorable day in 1963 when the Senate was debating
ratification of the nuclear test ban treaty. Speaking in support of that treaty, Senator Dirksen said, and I quote,

Under the circumstances, with bigger and more destructive
weapons being built all the time, with armament burdens upon
every country in the world, unless we take a step in the whole
domain of faith, what will be left except gloom and defeatism
against the day when some careless person will pull the trigger?

Everett Dirksen knew that somehow the peace of the
world must be made more secure, that if men had made
the world more dangerous, men could also make it safe
and had an obligation to make that effort. Twice in this
century, the whole world has gone to war. Twice, the
United States has joined the global struggle, believing with
Woodrow Wilson that "the right is more precious than
peace" and agreeing with Franklin Delano Roosevelt that
"we are willing to fight to maintain freedom."

Twice more we have honored our commitments to individual nations where peace was broken by acts of naked
aggression and by armies bent on destruction, terror, and
conquest. America has seen too much of war in the twentieth century, too much of suffering and dying on blood-
stained fields of battle.

We cherish the peace that America enjoys, the peace that

finds no Americans in combat anywhere in the world to-night. And yet, we know that the freedoms we have defended so often are being challenged today. We know that our strength, our power, our constant vigilance, and our resolve are the foundation of mankind's hope for peace and stability in the world.

If we should ever relinquish that role, if our contribution to peace should be diminished by our own weakness, the consequences could be severe and tragic for the whole world. For this reason, the United States must pursue a policy of peace through strength. That is the policy which my Administration will always pursue.

In the last nineteen months, I have taken affirmative action to ensure that America's alliances are strong, our commitments are worthwhile, and our defenses are without equal in the world.

In my presidency, I have proposed the two largest peacetime defense budgets in American history as the best assurance of deterring aggression and maintaining our own national security. There are some very sincere, very thoughtful, and very patriotic Americans who believe that these defense proposals take too much of our financial resources, take them away from domestic programs supported by the federal government. And I respect that view. But we must remember that the foundation for all of these domestic programs, the basic premise upon which they all depend is that the United States will continue as a free, independent, and secure nation. That must be our highest priority, and in this Administration, it is.

Beyond securing our own independence, America's defensive strength, by the very fact of its existence, enables us to deter aggression in many parts of the world. And that strength makes it possible for us to negotiate for peaceful progress from a position that commands respect and invites cooperation.

Because both sides of the Middle East conflict respect our strength, our word, and our commitment to a just and

lasting peace, we have won the role of a peacemaker in that very strategic and very volatile part of the world.

Our aim is to make peace secure throughout the world. We are conducting our foreign policy with our eyes open, our guard up, and our powder dry. We know that peace and national security cannot be pursued on a one-way street, but we also know that returning to a collision course in a thermonuclear age can leave the human race in ashes.

I will not lead the American people down the road to needless danger and senseless destruction. I will lead them on the path of peace through strength, and we will live in peace and freedom in the United States of America.

It is our duty and our great opportunity to make the most of the peace and freedom we enjoy in America today. Let us show ourselves worthy of the price we have paid for them in blood, in sacrifice, and in treasure.

Let us take more seriously and more personally our precious right of free political expression in this election year. Let us set ambitious goals for the future of our country and work hard and work together to achieve those goals.

Let us strive to secure the blessings of liberty for ourselves and our posterity and stand tall and strong and free among the nations of the world.

Let us make certain that the cause of freedom has no better friend, no stronger ally than the United States of America. And let us resolve, as the greatest son of Illinois did a century ago, that the "government of the people, by the people, and for the people, shall not perish from the earth."

I thank you, and now I would be delighted to answer any questions.

QUESTION: Mr. President, I'm from Godfrey, Illinois, and a student from Bradley University.

Many economists today feel that the country's economic problems are caused to a large degree by cost-push inflationary pressures rather than the more traditional demand-

pull pressures. In this context, what are your plans, if any, to break up the monopolistic tendencies of big business and big labor and their price-fixing abilities which tend to interfere with the efficient operation of the market?

THE PRESIDENT: About a year ago, I appointed an outstanding person to be our Attorney General, who was an expert in antitrust actions. Ed Levi, of the University of Chicago, served as an assistant attorney general in the Antitrust Division, some fifteen or twenty years ago. He is acknowledged as an expert in antitrust matters.

At his request, I have added to the number of antitrust lawyers in the Attorney General's Office. I can assure you that under his leadership there will be active, affirmative action taken to operate under the laws of the United States in antitrust actions.

In addition, about a year ago, I submitted to the Congress legislation that would add to the penalties in dollars—in criminal action, those who violate our antitrust laws. It seems to me that through this kind of action we can make certain, in the business world at least, that there will be a proper governmental role in making an environment where free enterprise can operate without a monopolistic development.

In the field of labor, I have been condemned and complimented for the fact that I vetoed the common situs picketing bill which had some ramifications involved in this overall area. The strength of our free enterprise system depends upon competition. We can't have big business, big labor—or big government, I might add—dominating our economy.

QUESTION: Thank you, Mr. President.

QUESTION: Mr. President, I'm a student at Bradley University from Spring Valley, New York.

In an announcement made two days ago, the Air Force informed Bradley University that our Air Force Reserve Officers Training Corps program will be closed down, ef-

fective in the spring of 1977. For the past twenty-seven years, through thick and thin, Bradley has supplied the Air Force with highly qualified personnel. The loss of this program will cause Bradley approximately a quarter of a million dollars annually.

In your opinion, Mr. President, is it possible for the Air Force to justify this action as a suitable reward for Bradley University's continuing support for over a quarter of a century?

THE PRESIDENT: Based on what you told me, I'm disgusted with the action of the United States Air Force. Quite frankly, it's incomprehensible, and we will do our darnedest to rectify the error. And I will let Dr. Abegg know. I just don't understand it. It sounds ridiculous.

QUESTION: Thank you very much, Mr. President.

QUESTION: Good evening, Mr. President, I'm from Ridgewood, New Jersey, and I'm also a student here at Bradley University.

Recently, Mayor Young, of Detroit, made statements expressing not only his city's fears, but also those of Philadelphia, San Francisco, and several other major cities concerning their somewhat suspect present financial stability and that of the future and also the ability to continue to provide for the necessary public services.

Has your Administration formulated a program to help prevent fiscal crises in other cities besides New York, prior to that crisis or, if not, will the tactics or methods used in New York's fiscal crisis also be used in other cities?

THE PRESIDENT: Of course, my Administration has strongly supported the general revenue sharing program, which gives to our states and to cities and to other local units of government about $6 billion a year which, in effect, is free for those cities to utilize as they see fit, for whatever programs or policies that they determine at the local level.

That's a good program; I fully support it. And in addi-

tion, we have many other categorical grant programs that go to state or local units of government. It seems to me, having been somewhat closely associated with the conflicts involved in the city of New York, that communities around the country have to learn that they have to manage their fiscal affairs in a responsible way.

We found that New York City, not for one year but for a period of time, had not handled its finances very responsibly. And the net result was they found that their expenditures, their receipts were in bad shape, that their cash flow problem was disastrous. I don't think we can permit other cities to expect that the federal government is going to bail them all out, because we aren't. If we can't establish responsibility at the local level and at the state level and at the federal level, we could go down the same disastrous path that some other countries—friends of ours—have gone down for the last twenty years. And as far as I am concerned, we're not going to permit it locally, statewide, or nationally.

QUESTION: Thank you, Mr. President.

QUESTION: Mr. President, I'm a senior at Bradley University. A recent national wire service reported that you have gained a lead over your opponent, Governor Reagan, in the upcoming Florida primary. One of the voter comments listed by the wire service favorably mentioned your performance in office to date, but expressed disfavor with your handling of the pardon granted to former President Richard M. Nixon.

I would like to know whether you are prepared to state unequivocally that there was no deal made between Secretary of State Kissinger, chief of staff General Haig and yourself, or any member of your staff in regard to resignation and subsequent pardon of former President Nixon?

If no such deal was agreed upon, would you please be willing to discuss your reasons for the granting of the pardon to Mr. Nixon?

THE PRESIDENT: In the first place, there was no deal made in any way, whatsoever. Categorically, no. And let me take you back, if I might, to the situation in July and August and September of 1974. This country had gone through a nightmare, a traumatic experience unprecedented in our country. And I became President under the most extraordinary circumstances—not because I sought the office, but because I had the opportunity to serve. And I found shortly after becoming President, that if we were to go through a long series of events that would have been, I think, extremely disturbing to the situation in our country, the better procedure would be to make a decisive decision and get the matter off our back so that we could handle our problems domestically with the economy and our problems internationally.

It was a decision made by me alone. Nobody else had any responsibility, good or bad. But we had to get on with the job of looking at our problems and solving them, both at home and abroad, and that had to be pushed aside so that all of us—215 million Americans—could concentrate on the future and forget the past, as bad as it was.

QUESTION: Thank you, Mr. President.

QUESTION: Good evening, Mr. President. I'm from North Belmont, New York, and a sophomore bio major here at Bradley.

Mr. President, you have come under fire lately by former Governor Reagan, former Governor Carter, and others, concerning the State Department's handling of détente. What is your justification for the foreign policy positions taken by your Administration in regard to the Soviet Union and China, in particular US-Soviet grain dealings, past and future?

THE PRESIDENT: Well, let me say very specifically that we are going to forget the use of the word *détente*. I said that back in August of 1975, when I spote to the American Legion in Minneapolis, Minnesota. The word is inconse-

quential. What happens in the negotiations between the United States and the Soviet Union, what happens in the negotiations between the People's Republic of China and the United States—those are the things that are of consequence.

Now this Administration believes that we have an obligation not to go back to the cold war where confrontation, in effect, took place literally every day of the year. We have an obligation to try and meet every problem individually, specifically, every issue as it comes up, in an effort to negotiate rather than to confront, whether it's with the Soviet Union or the People's Republic of China.

And we can do this effectively if we have the strength, militarily and otherwise, to have a two-way street. Now the United States, despite what some critics have said, has not under any circumstances gotten the short end of the deal. We're good Yankee traders, and we've done darn well by the United States.

Now let's take the grain sales to the Soviet Union. I know some candidates for the presidency have said that we ought to not make any sales, that we ought to buy all the grain from the farmers and store them in government-owned warehouses, put that heavy lid over the price structure of our agriculture at a cost, as it was some ten years ago, of $1 million a day, about $400 million a year. That's what it cost to store grain when we weren't selling it overseas. I just don't think we should make our farm export problem the pawn of the international politics. By strong, effective negotiation, we came out with a good agricultural deal with the Soviet Union.

And if we get a SALT Two agreement that will keep a lid on strategic arms in the next seven to ten years, it will be to the benefit of the United States. Let me ask this very simple question: Is it better to have a mutual limit of 2,400 launchers and 1,320 MIRV missiles—isn't that better than having 4,000 or 5,000 launchers or 2,000 or 4,000 MIRV missiles? Isn't that better for all of us? It really would be

better if we could go below 2,400 and 1,320 as long as we had rough equivalents between the two superpowers.

If we had an open themonuclear arms race, that's not in the best interest of the United States or the world as a whole. We have an obligation to have rough equivalency that will deter aggression, either by us or by them, and permit us to do some things that are needed and necessary for the world as a whole, as well as for the United States.

Any of these people that challenge us in these kinds of day-to-day negotiations, issue by issue, problem by problem, haven't been in the ballgame. They have lots of rhetoric, but I don't think they understand the problems.

QUESTION: Thank you very much, Mr. President.

QUESTION: Mr. President, I am a student at Bradley University. Mr. President, would you please state the criteria you used in the selection of Mr. Stevens as a Supreme Court Justice, and would you use the same criteria in the selection of future Supreme Court Justices?

THE PRESIDENT. I'm very proud of the selection of Supreme Court Justice Stevens. We went through a very constructive process of soliciting names from a wide variety of individuals or organizations that wanted to maintain a very high quality on our Supreme Court.

We had a number of highly qualified individuals. The Department of Justice solicited views from the American Bar Association. They interviewed, as I recall, some ten individuals whose names had been submitted to me. They came up with three or four that seemed to fit the requirements of the day and, after looking at the recommendations, the backgrounds, and all of the other qualifications, I came to the conclusion that Justice Stevens would be an outstanding member of the United States Supreme Court.

And I was delighted to see that a Democratic Congress, dominating the Senate by about or better than two to one, almost unanimously approved him. So I think we went through a good process. It was proven that he had the qual-

ifications to be an outstanding jurist, and that's what we want. And to the extent that I can do it in the future, that's exactly the process I will follow in the days ahead.

QUESTION: Thank you, Mr. President.

QUESTION: Good evening, Mr. President. I am from WWCT, here in the great city of Peoria. I'd like to ask you what significance Mr. Nixon's recent trip to China had, and has it in any way undermined your recent journey there several months ago?

THE PRESIDENT: Under no circumstances has that trip by Mr. Nixon, as a private citizen, invited as a private citizen by the People's Republic, undermined my trip to China, my negotiations with Chairman Mao and the other Chinese officials. Under no circumstances did it undercut, undermine, or interfere with the relations of our government with that government.

QUESTION: Good evening, Mr. President. I'm an economics major. Do you believe, with the present state of the economy, that tighter investment spending with the reduction of taxes will boost the economy to preinflationary levels?

THE PRESIDENT: Well I'm convinced that it's far better to give tax reductions to stimulate the economy, to increase employment and decrease unemployment, than to put programs through the Congress where you increase federal government spending and where you provide temporary employment for individuals, whether it's at the state or local level. That's the policy of this Administration, and that's one of the problems I have with the Congress. They want to go the other way. But we're going to fight them; we're going to win, because we are right.

QUESTION: Mr. President, I'm a journalism major from Bethany, Connecticut. My question is, Mr. President, what effect do you feel the Watergate incident will have on the

upcoming Presidential election? That is, do you feel that many Americans will vote Democratic because of Watergate?

THE PRESIDENT: I have no authoritative way of making an accurate determination on that. I can only say that I, as a candidate, had absolutely nothing whatsoever to do with Watergate, so it has no relationship to my background, my qualifications. I would hope that the performance of the last nineteen months would indicate that I have an Administration that's open; it's frank. It doesn't promise more than it can produce, and it won't lie to the American people under any circumstances.

These are the fundamentals by which my Administration has tried to operate. And everybody that works for me understands what those rules and regulations are. So we are different. We have no connection with Watergate. And so I would hope that the American people would look at me and those that work with me in that light, rather than remembering a sad and tragic past in American history.

QUESTION: Thank you, Mr. President.

QUESTION: Mr. President, I'm a resident of Peoria and a part-time student at Bradley. I wonder if you would clarify your position on the subject of civil rights for gay people in America.

THE PRESIDENT: Civil rights for what?

QUESTION: For gay people, with respect to hiring, employment, and housing. And secondly, if you were elected President, how would you hope to eliminate some of the discrimination that gay people in America live under?

THE PRESIDENT: I recognize that this is a very new and serious problem in our society. I have always tried to be an understanding person as far as people are concerned who are different than myself. That doesn't mean that I agree with or would concur in what is done by them or their position in society. I think this is a problem we have to face up to, and I can't give you a pat answer tonight. I just

would be dishonest to say that there is a pat answer under these very difficult circumstances.

QUESTION: Thank you very much.

QUESTION: Mr. President, I'm pastor of a church here in Peoria. From time to time we get reports, printed sometimes, to the effect that Mr. Kissinger and the State Department have already made promises and commitments regarding the Panama Canal to a government which is something less than friendly to us. And, furthermore, it has been suggested that the constitutional caution which forbids any United States property to be sold without approval of the Congress—that that will be circumvented by retaining title to it but nevertheless technically not selling it, but in reality giving all the controls and direction and jurisdiction to the Panama government, which only the owner of the property should have. I'd like you, Mr. President, to comment on that if you would.

THE PRESIDENT: Well first, let me say that whatever is done, if it reaches that point, will be fully submitted to the United States Congress, both the House as well as the Senate. If property is sold—and I'm not saying it is—or is transferred, it would have to be approved by both the House and the Senate and, of course, if it's a treaty, it would have to be approved by the Senate alone. So you can rest assured that whatever is done, if anything is done, will be submitted in its entirety and completely open and above board.

Now, the situation is that since 1964, when they had a series of riots in the Panama area—the Canal Zone and the Government of Panama—some thirty people were killed in these riots, including a significant number of Americans. Those circumstances precipitated negotiations that have been carried on by three Presidents. Those negotiations are going on today between the government of Panama and the United States.

I can only assure you—because the negotiations have not been completed—that the United States, as far as I am

concerned, will never give up its national defense interests nor give up its interests in the operation of the Panama Canal. And whatever is negotiated—and nothing has been concluded—will be submitted in its entirety to the Congress of the United States.

QUESTION: Thank you, Mr. President.

QUESTION: Good evening, Mr. President. I'm from Peoria. As you know, central Illinois has had a severe natural gas shortage. What do you propose to do about this natural gas shortage at a national level?

THE PRESIDENT: Let me thank you for asking one of the most fundamental questions asked here tonight. The United States is presently hamstrung by some outmoded legislation that precludes us from stimulating the production of more domestic natural gas production.

The Congress has been struggling for a long time. The Senate passed a good bill about two months ago. The House of Representatives, by a razor-thin, narrow margin, passed a bad bill—terrible, absolutely terrible—which is worse, in effect, than what we have as a matter of law right now.

Unfortunately, we are at a loggerhead or a stalemate. We have had a declining production within the United States of natural gas since 1973, and as long as the present law or the House of Representatives' bill are law, it will go down and down and down and down and we will buy more and more and more foreign Arab oil, and that's not good for America.

What I'm saying is, get the Members of the House of Representatives—I think all the ones here voted right—[*laughter*]—get them to help us to go along with the Senate and stimulate domestic production.

QUESTION: Mr. President, this will be the last question.

THE PRESIDENT: Can't we have one more? There is a nice-looking young lady over there. [*Laughter*]

QUESTION: Mr. President, I'm from Peoria and I'm a postal employee. I understand that you were against increasing the postal subsidy, and now they have been denied the chance to close the rural post offices. What do you see as the future for the Postal Service, a service that is vital to all Americans?

THE PRESIDENT: I think we're right down to the barebone facts. We either have to achieve greater economies in the operation of the Postal Service and have a smaller deficit, or we have to charge the people who use the Postal Service for the service that is rendered. Or if we don't achieve more economies in the operation or the people who use the Postal Service aren't going to pay more, then the taxpayers, as a whole, have to pay the deficit.

It's just one of three options. Now, I happen to believe we can do a better job running the Post Office. There is no reason in the world why the Post Office should have $1,300 million deficit in a twelve-month period. So we come right down to how we can eliminate the deficit, and there are three options. And I think the Congress has to work with me, but the people in the Post Office Department have to work with us in order to solve the problem.

QUESTION: Thank you.

QUESTION: Mr. President, before we let the last question go with the lovely lady, I'm the director of the Dirksen Endowment Fund, and on behalf of the Dirksen Congressional Research Center and, particularly, Louella Dirksen, we wish to thank you for your continued support to the Dirksen name and, particularly, to the Center. And I want to say tonight that you're not only playing well, you're going to continue to play well.

QUESTION: Thank you, Mr. President. I am from the city of Peoria. The Peoria *Journal Star* has reported that you have asked Congress for block grants for education at the

elementary and secondary level. These block grants would replace twenty-four aids-in-grants. This sounds great, but would you assure us that we would have less restrictions? Title I and some of the titles are extremely restrictive to us in the local area and to handling these funds.

THE PRESIDENT: You are exactly right. I have recommended to the Congress that we take twenty-four primary, secondary—or elementary and secondary—education categorical grant programs, consolidate them in one block grant program, and that the money should go to the states and to the local units of government without any matching requirement, so that at the local and state level, independent decisions could be made as to which areas there should be local emphasis.

The local emphasis in Peoria might be different than the legitimate needs and local emphasis in Miami, or the local emphasis or needs in Grand Rapids might happen to be different from what they are in San Francisco. So, the block grant program gives this flexibility. And we have promised every state and every local unit of government they will get no less money than they've gotten this current fiscal year, and they have much more decisionmaking responsibility at the local and the state level. The more we get education decisions made at the local level without court interference, the better off we are in this United States.

Could I say one final word. That's great music, but I've got a couple of more lines. [Laughter]

Obviously, I've enjoyed being at this outstanding University tonight and talking with all of you from Bradley as well as from Peoria and surrounding areas. But before I leave—you know a long time ago, I played football at the University of Michigan back when the ball was round, and I just have a great interest in athletics. I think it's great. I'm proud of it. I am proud of the fact that Bradley has done so well in basketball, and I'm a great enthusiast of Chet Walker. But before I leave, let me pay my respects to an-

other great product in Peoria, the basketball team at Rich-
woods High School.

And let me conclude my comments tonight by saying
that I would like nothing better than to follow their example and go undefeated in Illinois in 1976.

# THE ETHICS OF THE MARKETPLACE

## CAN FREE ENTERPRISE SURVIVE SUCCESS? [1]

### STANLEY MARCUS [2]

During the past year "an epidemic of corporate corruptions" has swept the country. Close on the heels of the Watergate scandal have come alarming disclosures of illegal political contributions, of bribery of officials in foreign countries, to get favorable contracts, of price fixing by major companies, and of questionable advertising strategies. The cases can no longer be excused as isolated instances. A survey by the Opinion Research Corporation of 531 upper and middle executives found that 48 percent condoned bribes abroad when the practices were prevalent in the foreign country. In other words, businessmen justified low ethical conduct because they had to compete with others with low ethics.

In the face of mounting distrust of business practices, prominent executives in increasing numbers have come forward to censure wrongdoing and corruption among their colleagues. Fred T. Allen, president of Pitney Bowes, recently made his position clear before the American Chamber of Commerce meeting in Switzerland. Suggesting the absolute necessity of firm standards, he said:

> I feel we should say to the public that we do not condone and will not make excuses for those who offend our sense of corporate morality. When we consider corporate morality, we must conclude that no price is too high, for the reality is that in the long run we have no alternative to ethical business behavior.

Thomas A. Murphy, chairman of General Motors Corporation, stressed the same theme before an audience at the University of Michigan (February 19, 1976):

> Just as political liberty is threatened when men in power violate the spirit of our constitutional freedoms, so is the economic freedom we enjoy under our free enterprise sys-

[1] Delivered to ABC Forum of the University of Nebraska at Omaha, November 18, 1975. Quoted by permission.

[2] For biographical note, see Appendix.

tem placed in jeopardy when a code of honesty and social responsibility is not honored by business men and women.

Charles H. Zeanah, director of corporate public relations of the Ethyl Corporation, speaking to a group of public relations men, was quoted by the Baton Rouge *Morning Advocate,* April 18, 1976:

> Business has a credibility problem and has failed to communicate effectively. It has grown too suspicious and antagonistic toward the media. . . . Business has lately become its own worst enemy and has been attacking the effect rather than the cause. Open communication is the best course of action. But in order to set in motion open communication, we have to get over our fear of the press.

Stanley Marcus, executive of Neiman-Marcus, the famous Dallas department store, addressed himself to this "massive loss of faith in the business community" in a speech to the ABC (Academy, Business, and Community) Forum, sponsored by the University of Nebraska at Omaha, November 18, 1975. He spoke to an audience of more than 620 persons. The ABC series is designed to present the views of thoughtful leaders and molders of opinion to the academic, business, and general communities in a forum setting which allows time for questions and answers after the formal presentation by the speaker of the day. These programs occur five times during the academic year as part of a 7:30 A.M. breakfast meeting in an off-campus community facility.

Charles R. Hein, director of university relations of the University of Nebraska at Omaha, reported: "The response as measured by applause, questions and requests for reprints, particularly from the corporate sector, was enthusiastic and large. Some portions of the Marcus address were reprinted in the New York *Times*" (Op-Ed page, December 15, 1975).

The speech was refreshing because the speaker met head-on the problem of business ethics. He was particularly lucid in analyzing the present situation and was specific in his indictment. He dismissed many of the rationalizations sometimes offered by businessmen. He declared that his purpose was "to preserve" the free enterprise system. His listeners were probably surprised to hear him endorse government regulation as a means of preserving competition. Near the conclusion he pulled his solution together when he said, "The success of free enterprise is predicated on certain rules: rules of competition, honesty, fairness, decency, truthfulness. And when businessmen won't play by those rules, the free

enterprise system is going to collapse and we're going to get socialism."

Those wishing to get another view of the problems of business ethics should read Stanley J. Goodman's speech "Raising the Fallen Image of Business" in REPRESENTATIVE AMERICAN SPEECHES, 1973-1974, p 160-75.

It's a very great pleasure for me to be here in Omaha today and to have the opportunity to address this distinguished group of business leaders. As a businessman myself —with nearly a half century of experience—I am going to exercise my "insider's prerogative" to indulge in some straight talk with you about a subject that is of great concern to us all.

We businessmen are in serious trouble in this country— and I am not referring to our current economic woes. We had problems before the bottom fell out of the economy, and we will have problems after the recovery, if things continue as they are. In that respect, we businessmen are like the rancher down in my part of the country who remarked to me one time that the Great Depression of the 1930s wouldn't have been so bad for him and his fellow ranchers *if it hadn't come right in the middle of hard times.*

Well, the particular "hard times" that you and I are in the middle of is a massive loss of faith in the business community by the American people—and perhaps a loss of faith on the part of businessmen as well.

I'm not telling you anything you don't already know: you read the opinion polls the same as I do. And they all tell us the same thing.

At the beginning of this decade of the 1970s, nearly 60 percent of the people expressed confidence in business: Today that figure has fallen below 30 percent. It has even a lower rating with young people. Only one out of seven of the eighteen- to twenty-year-olds express confidence in the way business is run. To me that means that the brightest and ablest of our young men and women are opting for other professions because they do not believe that business

can give them the sense of fulfillment and pride that they seek in their careers. And to me, that spells trouble for the entire business community.

Some people react to this with the response: "Oh, there'll always be people who want to make a buck." To which I reply: "God help us if those are the only people we can attract into business, if 'making a buck' is the only ideal that motivates young businessmen today."

But the attitude that concerns me most is the one which shrugs off this decline in public confidence in the mistaken belief that it is merely a part of a larger loss of confidence in *all* of our institutions.

Now, I will admit that business is not alone in its woes. Certainly government has suffered a loss of public confidence, as well as business. So have our universities. So have our doctors, our lawyers, and our military leaders. So have members of the press.

I will concede the point that the better educated the American people become, the more critical they become of the institutions that serve them. This is the *real* significance of the consumer movement. More is demanded of business than in years past.

But it is also clear that public discontent in almost every instance is fed by specific abuses within specific institutions.

People are down on politics because of Watergate and scandals on the local level, too numerous to mention.

People are down on government because even though government gets bigger, our problems never seem to get any smaller.

People are down on our universities because they don't like administrative indifference or their failure to incorporate ethical standards as part of all the educational process.

People are down on the military because of the misleading forecasts by US commanders in Vietnam.

People are down on the press because they do not perceive most of our reporters and newscasters as being fair

and unbiased. Headline sensationalism is one of the prices we pay for a free press, operating in free enterprise economy.

So let's not kid ourselves into believing that the negative attitude toward business is merely part of an "antiestablishment" mood throughout the nation. It is a lot more specific than that—and a lot more justified than that.

In my business—which depends so much on the good will of the people—I have always operated on the theory that "Where there's smoke, there's fire." If the reputation of Neiman-Marcus were to begin to slide, I wouldn't ask the local religious leaders if church and synagogue attendance had fallen off. I wouldn't ask the politicians if voter registration was down. I wouldn't even ask our competitors if their sales were sagging. I'd ask what *we* were doing at Neiman-Marcus to hurt our *own* reputation. I'd ask if the famous friendliness and courtesy of our service had fallen off, or if the quality of our merchandise had dropped.

Those are the kinds of questions that the entire business community should be asking itself today, rather than looking for excuses; rather than blaming a vague mood of public discontent.

Several years ago, the vice president in charge of public relations at one of the nation's major automobile manufacturers made a speech in Dallas. He began, much as I have begun, by talking about the loss of public confidence in American business. But then he proceeded to blame this loss of confidence on "antibusiness forces" that were "working overtime" to ruin our reputation—and on a "clouded public perception" of the competitive free enterprise system.

To restore that lost confidence, he called on the public relations and advertising professions to bring to the public an understanding of what our competitive enterprise system has done and can do for the people.

That analysis is interesting for several reasons.

*First,* it indicates a complete lack of understanding of the public relations function. Real public relations ought to try

to get at the heart of a problem; to find out what's causing the problem so that the cause can be corrected. All too often, however, public relations attempts to paper over the flaws while simultaneously trying to dazzle the public with a running account of all the good things that are going on.

*Second,* that analysis is a perfect example of the tendency we all have to look for scapegoats. Implied in that gentleman's statement is the belief that there are malicious, antibusiness devils behind the entire consumer movement. That's a dangerous assumption, as well as a naive one. It's sort of like blaming lung cancer on your doctor while you go on smoking. One of the biggest mistakes that Detroit ever made—and may still be making—was to assume that Ralph Nader was the father of the consumer movement, whereas, in reality, he was its child.

Let us not make a similar mistake. Our problems are not superficial. Nor can they be cured by superficial solutions.

To paraphrase Shakespeare, "The fault lies not in our press, dear friends, but in ourselves." And quite frankly, there is a good deal more at stake than our reputations. I believe the future of the entire free enterprise system may be at stake, as well.

I think you will agree that that is a rather profound concern.

Like each of you here today, I am a product of the free enterprise system. I know what it has meant, not just to me, but to this nation. I know that it is, by far, the most successful and most efficient economic system yet devised by the mind of man.

Like democracy, free enterprise is not perfect, but it is the best there is. You remember Winston Churchill's comment on democracy. "It has been said that democracy is the worst form of government—except all those other forms that have been tried from time to time." That describes free enterprise as well.

Free enterprise has made the United States the richest,

most productive and most powerful nation in history. And, despite some of our obvious shortcomings, that system has given us the highest standard of living in history as well.

I want to preserve that system. I want my grandchildren and *their* grandchildren after them to enjoy the same opportunities that I have had and you have had. That is why I am here today; to express to you some of the concerns I have about the future. In my recent book, *Minding the Store,* I described myself as "A 'progressive' who believes so strongly in the principles of the free enterprise system that I recognize the necessity for constant reform and improvement to save the system from itself."

Let's be honest with ourselves about this whole matter. The public isn't down on business, as such. Americans still believe in the free enterprise system. They have no quarrel with profit-making.

But, they do have a quarrel with unethical and questionable business practices conducted at the public expense.

They do have a quarrel with companies which pollute our water and air and are apparently indifferent to the hazards of pollution until the government intervenes.

They do have a quarrel with that majority of businessmen who have fought and obstructed and delayed every piece of progressive legislation enacted during this century. Who among the business community today would seriously propose that Congress repeal our child labor laws—or the Sherman Antitrust Act? The Federal Reserve Act, the Security Exchange Act? or workmen's compensation? or Social Security? or minimum wage? or Medicare? or civil rights legislation? All of us today recognize that such legislation is an integral part of our system; that it has made us a stronger, more prosperous nation—and, in the long run, has been good for business. But we can take precious little credit for any of the social legislation now on the books, for business vigorously opposed most of this legislation—and we *get* precious little credit from the people. As Stanley Goodman, chairman of the May department stores, commented, "It's

all the same story, business trying to hold the clock back and the legislation passing anyway."

I wonder sometimes if we really believe in the free enterprise system. When those who have the greatest stake in it often turn out to be its greatest enemies, I wonder if free enterprise can survive.

Can it survive when some of its greatest proponents seem determined to strangle the life force of the system—*competition*—with such practices as collusive bid rigging and price-fixing? The list of the guilty reads like an honor roll of Standard and Poor: Allis-Chalmers . . . Federal Pacific Electric . . . General Electric . . . General Motors . . . McKesson & Robbins . . . Parke-Davis . . . Joseph E. Seagram & Sons . . . Westinghouse. Those companies ought to be the showcase of competition, not its enemy.

Can free enterprise survive inaccurate, misleading, or "unexplained" financial reporting? Or auditors who violate their code of ethics to help companies like Equity Funding falsify its financial statements and perpetrate a massive swindle, running into the hundreds of millions of dollars, that involved inflated assets, sales and earnings, fraudulent insurance policies, nonexistent securities, and the collection of death benefits on coverage that never existed? What are we to think—not just of the executives behind the fraud and the auditors who helped them—but of the dozens of employees who knew about the fraud but did nothing, and the powerful investors who benefited from the inside information?

Can free enterprise survive companies which flout the law by making illegal political contributions with corporate funds? Is it any wonder that 53 percent of our population believes that the large corporations should be broken up when they read that in 1972 seven companies alone contributed nearly a half million dollars to the Committee to Re-elect the President: American Airlines, Ashland Oil, Gulf Oil, Goodyear, 3-M, Phillips Petroleum and Braniff Airways? It does no good to try to justify these contributions—as some

have done—as the cost of doing business with the government. Other companies *refused* to give—and they're still in business.

Now, I'm not so naive as to suggest that business is any more corrupt than it ever was. It might even be less so.

I am well aware of the fact that the twin movements of consumerism and reform have put the spotlight of publicity on business wrongdoing, and have also conditioned the public to expect a higher standard of ethics from business at all levels.

I also recognize that communications have improved so vastly that a crime committed in Duluth becomes known in Dallas the night it is discovered. Fifty years ago, it might have taken the people of Dallas six months to learn that such a crime was even committed. So I don't think that business is worse. It's just that our flaws show up much faster today than they used to.

But that is small comfort when we continue to read about shoddy products or services which do not live up to their claims. Or when the people become victims of false or misleading advertising, poor service, unnecessary repairs, or meaningless warranties.

It is certainly small comfort when we are treated to fresh revelations, almost daily, about American corporations spending hundreds of millions of dollars overseas in political contributions, bribery, payoffs, and so-called agent fees. Businessmen who have been involved in these practices argue that they are traditional business customs locally and are necessary to compete with foreign business firms; necessary for Northrop to sell airplanes in the Middle East . . . for Exxon to do business in Italy . . . for United Brands to do business in Honduras . . . for Gulf Oil to do business in Bolivia.

They also argue that many of the payments are perfectly legal, in a technical sense.

Maybe so, but in my judgment, those practices pose a great moral dilemma for our nation in general and for the

American business community in particular. Our culture is based on the Judeo-Christian code of ethics which espouses lofty moral standards of fair and honest dealing. Now, however, we seem to have revised those standards. We still talk about dealing honorably and forthrightly with people. But we're now saying that we believe in this credo domestically, but it doesn't count overseas. In other words, to hell with the foreigner; we insist on honest scales at the supermarket but not for overseas shipments of grain.

I don't believe we can get away with that. I don't believe a double standard works, whether you're an individual, a corporation, or a nation. Sooner or later, your right hand becomes affected by what your left hand is doing. How long is it before we start asking ourselves: "Well, it works overseas; why not try it at home"? Is it already happening? Is it just coincidence that some of the companies which have admitted illegal political contributions overseas have also admitted to the same practice here at home?

So I reject the voices which defend unethical American business practices abroad. I reject the cynical attitude of former Treasury Secretary John Connally who said recently that too many US enterprises overseas have had to use "fang and claw" to operate because the US State Department gives them little or no support. When Mr. Connally tries to tell us that it is time to "curb the insidious feeling of guilt" over the problems of the world, I ask him what else but guilt—and alarm—are we supposed to feel as we watch the United States adding to those problems on a daily basis.

America is supposed to stand for something special in this world. We're not supposed to get down in the mud with the other nations; we're supposed to be a beacon for other nations to follow.

Our behavior is *supposed* to be different; that's what the American ideal is all about. Our credo should not be, "When in Rome, do as the Romans do." Rather, it should be, "When in Rome, do as Americans are supposed to do."

I think, by and large, we *have* stood for something special

in the world. I think we have earned the respect of the people of the world, except when we have violated our own code of ethics.

How do I answer those who say that payola is sometimes necessary to do business overseas? My anwer is that you have to *pay* for a code of ethics; *and* it doesn't come cheap. Our own company decided against entering a profitable foreign market when it became apparent that we would be subjected to a pay-off system as the price of admission.

And, again, I ask the question whether the free enterprise system can survive such abuses?

Do we really still believe in the free enterprise system when we treat competition as if it were poison? Competition is fuel that makes free enterprise work. Without it, free enterprise becomes corporate enterprise—and there is no corporation in the world that is wise enough to correct its internal mistakes. Competition has a way of correcting them very quickly and very effectively.

Over the years, governmental regulations came into being because of the failure—or inability—of business to regulate itself. For the most part, these regulations did not represent an indictment of business as a whole. They were designed to curb the abuses of a few—and in that sense, had the effect of protecting not only the public, but honest businessmen, as well.

Unfortunately, most businessmen have a paranoia about government regulations—and like all paranoia, it has no basis in fact. Mention the word *regulation* to a typical businessman, and I can give you a checklist of his predictable response:

☐ red tape
☐ bureaucratic bungling
☐ socialism
☐ unwarranted government interference
☐ strangling free enterprise
☐ big-brotherism
☐ controlled economy

Mix in a few profanities and take your choice.

Now another voice enters the debate. Now the President of the United States comes to us with his own brand of political soothsaying and tells us just what we want to hear: that we were right all along; government regulation of business is horrible—un-American—and that the government ought to get out of the regulation business. Let the free marketplace work. Oh, it sounds wonderful. And besides that, it's good politics.

And we nod our heads enthusiastically, almost drooling at the prospect of arriving at that millennium when every businessman can do as he damn well pleases; when all regulations will be declared null and void.

All of them?

Do we really want to eat meat that hasn't been inspected by a federal agency?

Or use an airline that isn't controlled by FAA flight regulations?

Or drive on city streets that don't have any stop lights?

Or buy drugs that have not been tested and approved by a Food and Drug Administration?

Or get on an elevator that hasn't been inspected in ten years?

Let's not be simplistic about this whole matter of regulation. Let's understand what we're talking about.

The fact is that regulation is not just some monster dreamed up by twentieth century advocates of big government. Regulation of commerce was one of the few specific domestic powers that our wise Founding Fathers reserved for the federal government in the Constitution. The interstate commerce clause of Article I provides that: "The Congress shall have power . . . to regulate commerce with foreign nations, *and* among the several states. . . ." Regulations sometimes get twisted around to the point that they *protect* some industries from competition, and attempts to deregulate are fought by the industries themselves.

The more complex and impersonal our society became,

the more regulations were required; and the stronger our partnership with government became.

Former Supreme Court Justice Abe Fortas observed recently that

> The nature of the problems to which government must respond has changed—and changed profoundly. The primary role of government has expanded far beyond that of the maker and enforcer of rules of conduct within which people freely operate. It is a participant in our daily lives, not merely an umpire. It has been burdened with the affirmative responsibility for assuring *minimum* standards of life and living. Its social obligation is no longer optional. It is a political and institutional imperative.

There is no doubt that the vast majority of Americans share this view—and we're just kidding ourselves if we think otherwise. While it is true that 91 percent of the public feels that the government should not own or run big business, 74 percent do want increased regulation of major companies and industries to be sure they don't take advantage of the public.

I agree that unwarranted regulation should be eliminated. There is no doubt that greater efforts should be made to assure that administrative decisions and procedures are fair. We do need mandatory, periodic, and comprehensive reviews of regulations to scrape off the barnacles that have accumulated and to reset the course of the regulations towards the goal of their original purposes. This is not a plea for more bureaucracy but *better!*

But let's face the obvious fact that regulation is a necessary part of our modern society and is always going to be with us. We don't add much to our credibility as business leaders by refusing to admit that fact.

But having said that, I hasten to add that government regulation of business will never take the place of *self*-regulation. Government regulation is for the unscrupulous few. Self-regulation is for the conscientious majority.

The success of free enterprise is predicated on certain rules: rules of competition, honesty, fairness, decency,

truthfulness. And when businessmen won't play by those rules, the free enterprise system is going to collapse and we're going to get socialism.

It's as simple as that.

Woodrow Wilson once remarked that, "The highest and best form of efficiency is the spontaneous cooperation of a free people."

For us, in the world of business, such cooperation—self-discipline, if you will—has become more than just a prerequisite for efficiency; it has become an absolute necessity for our survival.

# IDEALISM: WHAT'S WRONG WITH IT? [3]

## MARY JEAN PARSON [4]

The more intense the *competition* in business, in politics, in education, the more likely the *breakdown* in *moral* behavior.

That's the most chilling *"consensus"* I believe I've ever read. Because it strikes at the very heart of American society . . . competition.

This startling statement posed in stark terms a proposition that is bothering business, for it struck at a central tenet of the free enterprise system. This proposition plunged Mary Jean Parson into a frank discussion of business ethics in a speech delivered to the New York State Broadcasters Association Annual Executive Conference, held at Cooperstown, New York, July 14, 1975. Among her listeners were most of the owners and managers of broadcast stations in the state.

Parson was well known to her listeners. She is an effective communicator, having had considerable experience as a writer, as a theatre administrator, and as a unit manager, supervisor of program unit managers, manager of news program controllers, and at present director of planning, devolopment, and administration of ABC Leisure Group, which operates ABC theatres and amusement attractions. She has served as president of the New York City chapter of American Women in Radio and Television.

The speech was much in tune with what executives are commencing to say about morality and ethics (see speech by Stanley Marcus, above). J. Irwin Miller, chairman of the board of the Cummins Engine Company of Indiana and a deeply religious man, has said, "Business has spectacularly abused its freedom." He suggested that if business does not regulate itself it will invite government intervention:

It will suffer a new wave of legal restrictions if it does not curb itself voluntarily. But at the moment it is reacting to individual incidents and not taking a fresh look. It's generally defensive and not self-critical.

[3] Delivered to the New York State Broadcasters Association Annual Executive Conference, New York, July 14, 1975. Quoted by permission.
[4] For biographical note, see Appendix.

If you have a complex interdependent society like ours, it's like people jammed in an elevator. You can't swing your elbows everywhere. We in business must exercise restraint— or it will be imposed.

We must do less than the law allows and more than it requires. (Quoted by Charlotte Saikowski in the *Christian Science Monitor*, April 1976)

The speech fell clearly into a four-step development with an attention-getting introduction (about 300 words), the problem step (about 1,000 words), a solution (400 words), and finally a brief one-paragraph appeal for action. Skillfully, the speaker disarmed her listeners before she gave them the strong medicine touching their ethics. Wisely paraphrasing the Declaration of Independence, she suggested "equality, honesty, duty and love . . . to be ideas worth selling" and urged that we "dedicate ourselves to that effort in our nation's Bicentennial Year."

The successful inspirational speaker must avoid being accused of being tediously or pretentiously moralistic. Parson recommended that her fellow broadcasters attempt to communicate values to their listeners, but adroitly she implied that they apply the same virtues in their own business operations.

The title of my talk today is probably guaranteed to fill the golf course before lunch. Because of *course* we're all idealists. Pragmatic idealists, many of us. Idealistic pragmatists, many more. But like patriotism and motherhood, idealism just isn't talked about much any more. We talk about sex a good deal . . . even teach it in the schools. And I've not heard anybody knock apple pie lately. But we don't talk about idealism much anymore.

I don't think I'm betraying a trust when I give you a brief rundown of how this title evolved. I was called and invited to speak to you again this year, and in the course of the conversation I was told, "We'd rather you didn't talk about Affirmative Action this year. We all know our legal obligations and we don't need to hear about it again."

In truth, I suppose I could let your employment numbers speak for themselves, and let *you* decide if there's a need to talk about Affirmative Action anymore.

However . . . I said, "What *would* you like me to talk about?"

I was told, "Try to do something thought-provoking, not just a presentation. Give us something with an unusual perspective on life. Enlarge our horizons. What do you think?"

My first thought was, "At 10:30 in the morning?!" But my *response* was, "You sound like an idealist."

Quick as a wink, he came back, "What's wrong with idealism?"

Well, I allowed as how nothing was wrong with it, and I'd get back to him with my answer.

And then I began to think, what *is* wrong with idealism? Nothing. Except we don't hear much about it anymore.

And in this industry, in this time in our lives, as a people and as individuals, perhaps we'd *better* start talking about it again. Exploring it. Weighing it. *Is* it, like some folks say about God, dead? Or is it somewhere around the corner, waiting to be invited again, into our homes, into the board rooms, into the smoke-filled rooms, into our consciousness?

You know how it is when you start thinking about someone, the phone rings and they're on the line? Or you start thinking about an idea and you encounter it in everything you read?

Or you start talking with somebody about something that's been troubling you, and you find out *they've* been thinking about it too?

That's what I hope happens with us today.

A convocation was held at Yale recently, between alumni and the graduate and professional schools, discussing many areas of society's concerns. One panel discussed Professional Responsibility and Ethics. Charles W. Powers, an associate professor in the Divinity School, Robert Stevens of the Law School, and John E. Smith of the Philosophy Department conducted the forum. There was a consensus of the panel that competition has a correlation with honesty: the more intense the competition in business, in politics, in education, the more likely the breakdown in moral behavior.

I'll read that again . . . the more intense the *competition* in business, in politics, in education, the more likely the *breakdown* in *moral* behavior.

That's the most chilling *"consensus"* I believe I've ever read. Because it strikes at the very heart of American society . . . competition.

We're taught to compete from the time we're children. In fact, recent social scientists have postulated that one of the reasons men have a better chance than women of succeeding in the business world, is that they play competitive games as little boys, while little girls play supportive games, like dolls and nurse.

And yet a group of respected thinkers, representing religion, philosophy and law can blandly say . . . the more intense the competition in business, in politics, in education, the more likely the breakdown in moral behavior.

Can anyone of us here say them nay?

I think not.

When we read that the chairman of a distinguished corporation asserts that bribery of foreign officials is "a way of life" if a company wants international business.

When the number of lawyers involved in that swamp called Watergate is enough to boggle the mind, and to make one wonder if *any* ethics courses are taught in law schools anymore.

When the abuses of the Medicare and Medicaid systems soar into the millions of dollars, as insurance companies make illegal profits off the illnesses of our citizens.

When organized crime can publicly, and evidently with impunity, cooperate, and, indeed, work *for* a secret agency of the federal government.

When doctors go on strike, endangering the lives of thousands, to protest the bilking they are taking from insurance companies for malpractice insurance premiums; instead of attacking the real problem of an elitist AMA which keeps the *number* of doctors low, the *prices* of medical care high,

the hours *long,* and the incidence of *real* medical mistakes growing.

When a Supreme Court, after nearly two hundred years, finally decides that price-fixing by lawyers is a violation of more recent antitrust laws, and finally strikes down the practice.

In our own industry, in the forgettable fifties, when payola for DJ's was rampant, and giving answers to quiz-show contestants was practiced, all in the name of the almighty mass audience. Ratings! Shares!

In your own lives, when you take junkets . . . complete with family . . . at the expense of a station advertiser or supplier. Do you ever think twice about it?

When you turn down a Black or a Puerto Rican for a job at your station, because he "wouldn't fit in." Do you ever think about it?

When you pay a woman less than you'd pay a man for the same job, because "she doesn't need to work." Do you ever think about it?

When you send Nick Zapple, late of the Senate Communications Subcommittee, a case of booze, and your license just *happens* to be up for renewal this year. Do you ever think about it?

It appears that, indeed, competition *does* cause a breakdown in moral behavior in our society's business world. And we shrug our shoulders and say, "That's business." "What does that dame know about business?"

Let's talk about our personal conduct in the business world for a moment.

If you're the station engineer, and you were buying a new piece of equipment this year, how many companies romanced you? How many took you and your wife out to dinner? Which one handed you cash when he shook your hand one day? Who did you buy from?

If you're program director at a radio station, when was the last time a record company representative contacted you to offer you free tickets to a concert, or an invitation to a

special party, or a "free-lance promotion fee" for helping raise a record on the charts in your area?

If you're the news director, did you ever get invited to accompany a special press party . . . a governor, a President, a secretary of state? Did being an "insider" make you more receptive to the press handout, or did you retain your skepticism and ask hard questions? Did you attribute the party line to an "anonymous source," or did you give the real person's name in your story?

If you're a station manager, have you served with the Chamber of Commerce, the Mayor's Council, or on boards of other corporations? When you meet with the "leaders" of the community . . . the politicians, the bankers, the real estate interests, the union leaders . . . do you come to understand their point of view? And with that understanding, do you tacitly ignore the graft, the corruption, the deals, which we all know mar the lives of the people in your community, *your* constituency, your *audience?*

These are hard questions. They're not pleasant, and they're not meant to place blame. They're questions we have to ask. Not of each other. But of ourselves.

And it's not enough to accept the panacea that society has gone wrong. We must look at the tools of our trade, to see if we use or abuse their power.

Marshall MacLuhan has made a powerful and popular case that radio and television are vastly different tools. The nature of their impact and the differences in their influence are remarkable.

And now a new theorist has appeared on the scene, to explore the almost Pirandellian influence of television. He explores the question of where does reality end and fantasy begin. Not in the *content* of television programming . . . although there is an ocean of territory to be explored in that area . . . but in the *tool* itself.

Tony Schwartz is the author of the book, *The Responsive Chord.* Mr. Schwartz's insights have peculiar power, because he created the ill-famed political commercial for the 1964

Presidential campaign, which showed a child innocently picking daisy petals, one after another, as a countdown for a hydrogen bomb blast. Though there was no mention of the presidential candidate at whom the message was aimed, the effect of the commercial was so unnerving that its sponsoring party withdrew it after a few showings. Schwartz appears then to have some credentials for this theory.

Gutenberg man . . . the human race which has learned to read linearly, left to right, line by line, has lived by a communication system requiring the laborious coding of thought into words and then the equally laborious task of decoding by the receiver . . . i.e. . . . the reader. . . .

Electronic man . . . the generations we're rearing now . . . dispenses with this by communicating experience without the need of symbolic transformations. . . . He says, "In communicating at electronic speed, we no longer direct information *into* an audience but try to evoke stored information *out* of it in a patterned way."

Schwartz believes that the *totality* and *instantaneousness* of television, more than its *program content,* contributes, for instance, to more violence in society.

His premises lead him to the shattering conclusion that "*truth* is a *print* ethic, not a standard for *ethical* behavior in *electronic* communication." We must now be concerned not with Gutenberg-based concepts of *truth,* but with the *effects* of electronic communication.

So perhaps it's a matter of what you see *too much of,* is what you *come* to *dislike.* Familiarity breeds contempt. Or, perhaps it's a more fearful conclusion. Perhaps we're becoming observers to life, not participants; the *eternal audience.* We'd rather watch football on Sunday afternoon, than go out and get some exercise. We'd rather watch somebody make a statement at the voting booth, rather than go out ourselves and vote.

So it's a fundamental question: is it real, or is it fiction? Is it truth, or is it the illusion of truth? And make no mistake . . . if it is illusion . . . then it certainly isn't truth.

So we have two dilemmas . . . two recent theories which offer those of us in broadcasting perplexity. We are told that intense competition . . . the cornerstone of American society . . . undoubtedly causes a breakdown in moral behavior. And we are told that at least one of the tools we use in our industry . . . television . . . is in, and of itself, a possible enemy of truth to the audience which views it.

Some of you are now saying, what the hell is she talking about? We're in this business to make money. We operate in the public interest, we keep the community happy, we don't offend the FCC, and we sell as much advertising as we can. And that's *it!* Without a profit, we're out of business. Without advertisers, none of us would be here. And what's all this nonsense about truth and illusion? About competition . . . and ethics?

Well, that's exactly what I'm talking about. We are a *competitive, electronic, communications medium.* What you see . . . and what you hear . . . is what you get.

We are the greatest *selling* tool in the history of humanity. We can sell anything . . . Horizon property in the middle of the desert . . . Preparation H . . . or a presidential candidate. If this industry decides to sell something . . . the American public buys it . . . and ultimately the entire world buys it.

So I'm talking about a selling campaign. I'm talking about the most influential industry in the world . . . us . . . broadcasting . . . deciding to sell some *ideas.* We can sell *any*thing if we set our minds to it. As we enter our Bicentennial year . . . which celebrates our Revolution, by the way, not our freedom. That didn't come until 1783. But two hundred years ago, in 1775, a revolutionary idea was spawned and a Declaration of Independence was born. I would like to propose another revolutionary idea. I would like to propose a Declaration of Independence for Broadcasters.

And . . . in the America I have described, they are quite independent of the present drift of American society. If, as an Association, we can believe in this; if we can cause other

colleagues in our industry, to pause, to think, to join us; if we can dedicate ourselves for one year, as individuals and as a group, to the following propositions, we can change the world. We can sell *anything*; why not sell *ideas?* Why not make fools of those professors at Yale, and prove that the power of broadcasting can alter the ethical and moral behavior of those who hear us and see us. So here goes. Are the following ideas worth . . . as our forefathers once said . . . our lives, our fortunes, and our sacred honor?

We, the Broadcasters of the United States, in order to insure a more perfect society, declare these truths to be self-evident:

1. That *equality* is an idea worth *selling.* That all persons are entitled to equal treatment under the law, whether it be in job opportunity, housing accommodations, schooling, or equal pay for equal work. And that all citizens are entitled to mutual respect, one of another, and shall be treated that way, and shown that way, by broadcasters.

2. That *honesty* is an idea worth *selling.* That individual honesty, in word and deed, is the bedrock of corporate honesty, governmental honesty, societal honesty. That "the rules of the game" begin at home, in our day-to-day dealings as individuals, and that as broadcasters we will tell the truth, cut the pay-offs and risk the consequences.

3. That *duty* is an idea worth *selling.* That all persons are endowed by their Creator with certain inescapable duties, and that among those duties are work, learning and the pursuit of responsibility; that our attitude toward work determines our relationships with others; that a willingness to learn, meaning an open mind both to the new and the old, is necessary to keep liberty real; that a sense of responsibility to the future as well as to the present is necessary for real happiness. And as broadcasters, we will live, as well as broadcast, our duties of work, learning and responsibility.

4. That *love* is an idea worth *selling.* That a person need love the earth and all its inhabitants, the Creator of the

mystery, and one person more than life itself, to have experienced truly that wonderment called living. And that any program, any station break, any commercial, broadcast without that fullness and wisdom called love, shall be banned from *our* air waves.

We declare these ideas: equality, honesty, duty and love . . . to be ideas worth selling . . . and dedicate ourselves to that effort in our nation's Bicentennial Year.

I invite all of you to join me in this Declaration of Independence. To adopt it, to mean it, to live it, to broadcast it. If we did . . . we have the power to change the world.

# ANSWERS FROM ACADEMIA

## COWBOYS, INDIANS, AND THE LAND OF PROMISE: THE WORLD IMAGE OF THE AMERICAN FRONTIER [1]

### RAY A. BILLINGTON [2]

Many scholars of history and literature have drawn our attention to the importance of the social myth or what Henry Nash Smith has called "an intellectual construction that fuses concept and emotion into an image" (*Virgin Land: The American West as Symbol and Myth,* Harvard University Press, 1970). In his book, Smith has discussed at length the myths that have grown up around the West. Leo Marx has traced the influence that the garden myth has had on the westward movement in America (*The Machine in the Garden: Technology and the Pastoral Ideal in America,* Oxford University Press, 1964). Richard Hofstadter has talked about the agrarian myth (*The Age of Reform: From Bryan to F.D.R.,* Knopf, 1955). Anyone who has lived in the South has heard often about the Old South, the Lost Cause, White Supremacy, and the New South.

Billington presented the keynote address at the XIV International Congress of Historical Sciences, meeting at the Masonic Auditorium, San Francisco, August 22, 1975. In attendance were about two thousand scholars from throughout the world.

The International Congress of Historical Sciences assembles every five years. The meeting in 1975 was the first held in the United States. In 1970 it convened in Moscow, and in 1980 it will meet in Romania.

Professor Ray Billington, senior research associate of the Huntington Library and a distinguished historian, has drawn our attention to the pervasiveness of cowboys, Indians, and the Wild West as symbols far beyond the boundaries of the United States. He has produced an exciting lecture that is sound in its construction and analysis, full of enlightening thoughts, and at the

[1] Delivered at XIV International Congress of Historical Sciences at 3:00 P.M. August 22, 1975, Masonic Auditorium, San Francisco. Quoted by permission of Dr. Billington and Richard Schlatter, executive director of International Congress of Historical Sciences.

[2] For biographical note, see Appendix.

same time highly entertaining. It will, no doubt, have appeal to historians and popular readers alike.

The response to the address was highly favorable. Senator Barry Goldwater (Republican, Arizona) read it into the *Congressional Record* (March 9, 1976). It appeared in *Dialogue,* the United States Information Agency magazine, in the Bicentennial package sent out by the USIA. It has been translated into French, Spanish, Italian, German, and Russian.

I am sure that most of you will agree when I say that the "Wild, Wild West" is alive and well in much of the world today, nearly a century after the last cowboy blazed a path of virtue across the Great Plains with his six-shooters, and the last Apache unleashed his arrows against the encircled wagon train. For the myth of the American frontier as a land of romance, violence, and personal justice has persisted and grown, to influence popular attitudes toward the United States and its policies down to the present.

The persuasive influence of the frontier image is nowhere better exhibited than by the cultists of other nations who try to recapture life in that never-never land of the past. In Paris western addicts buy "outfits" at a store near the Arch of Triumph called the Western House, spend weekends at Camp Indien clad in Comanche headdresses and moccasins, or don cowboy sombreros and spurred boots to gallop through the Bois de Boulogne—on Vespas. Frontier buffs have brought affluence to the late George Fronval, a novelist who has written nearly six hundred westerns, fifty-four of them about "Buffalo Bill" Cody, under such improbable titles as *The Cavern of the Mammoths* and *The Prisoner of the Ku Klux Klan.*

In Austria children play Cowboys and Indians, or walk Indian File through the cobbled streets, their makeshift costumes contrasting strangely with half-timbered houses. In West Germany enthusiasts buy Rodeo After Shave and a deodorant called Lasso, purchase western clothes from two thriving chain stores (some buffs refuse to watch westerns on television unless properly garbed), and belong to one of

the sixty-three societies in the Western Clubs Federation whose members spend weekends in log houses, dress as Sioux Indians or cowboys, and carry realism to the uncomfortable extreme of using saddles for pillows and barring Indian impersonators from the club saloon. In Norway a "western" author, Morgan Kane, is a national hero among the young; in Japan "Frontier" restaurants vie for customers, and a *Frontier* magazine has recently appeared.

So irresistible is the compulsion to imitate western heroes that a Glasgow health officer not long ago lamented that Scottish lads were becoming round shouldered and hollow chested from copying the slouching stride of cowboys. Blue jeans transcend international boundaries in their appeal, even though, as in the Soviet Union they cost a full month's pay and authentic Levis even more. Nor do elders set a different example; when Party Leader Leonid I. Brezhnev visited former President Nixon in 1973 the one person he greeted with bear-hug enthusiasm was Chuck Connors, the hero of a television series called "The Rifleman."

All are responding to the image of the American West projected by twentieth century films, novels, and television programs: a sun-drenched land of distant horizons, peopled largely by scowling bad men in black shirts, villainous Indians, and those Galahads of the Plains, the cowboys, glamorous in hip-hugging Levis and embroidered shirts, a pair of Colt revolvers worn low about the waist. A land, too, of the shoot-out, individual justice, and sudden death at the hand of lynch mobs. A few months ago an Israeli army psychologist, pleased that his country's soldiers did not use their guns when on leave, expressed delight that "There is no shooting like in the Wild West."

That such an image should be popular today is easy to understand. To empathize with a make-believe land of masculinity and self-realization is to forget momentarily the monotony of a routinized machine civilization, to escape the uncertainties of a turbulent world, and to recapture an unregimented past. The vogue of a "Western" cult demon-

strates a universal urge to lessen the controls necessary in today's societies.

To understand that vogue is relatively easy; to trace the genesis of the frontier image demands a more extended analysis. Images do not emerge overnight, nor are they unrelated to the experiences of their holders. Instead they customarily define the past in terms of today's values, and evolve in directions governed by the psychological needs of the present. How, then, has the frontier image now current been shaped by prior experiences and modified to meet modern emotional needs?

The modern concept of the American West blends two different images that emerged during the eighteenth and nineteenth centuries. One pictured the frontier as lawless, brutal, and repelling, molded by a savage environment that reduced the frontiersmen to semibarbarism. The other painted the West as a transplanted Eden, overflowing with the bounties of nature, and beckoning the dispossessed to a new life of abundance and freedom. How and why did these conflicting images emerge and blend during the nineteenth century?

The myth of the frontier as a land of violence and lawlessness was the invention primarily of imaginative novelists and prejudiced travelers. The travelers who visited the West during the late eighteenth and nineteenth centuries can be counted by the hundreds; more than fifty of their accounts were published in Germany in the thirty years after 1815, over two hundred in England, nearly forty in Japan after 1868, dozens in France and Italy, eight in Hungary. The picture they painted was shaped by political bias; conservatives exaggerated the brutalizing impact of frontier democracy on men and institutions, while liberals overstressed the virtues of manhood suffrage and social equality. Both, however, were shocked by the crudities of western life, and the contrast between the cultural sophistication of their homelands and the primitive societies they encountered on the borderlands.

Even more influential than travelers as image-makers were novelists. James Fenimore Cooper set the example; his *Leatherstocking Tales* about the New York frontier took Europe by storm; they were translated into a dozen languages, sold hundreds of thousands of copies, and continue to be read today; in Russia alone thirty-four editions of Cooper's collected works have been published, two of them since 1917. Such popularity inspired imitation and in Cooper's wake a host of novelists turned to the American West as a scene for their adventures.

To single out a few of the giants of the trade is to do an injustice to dozens more: In England, Mayne Reid and Percy St. John; in France, Gustave Aimard and Gabriel Ferry; in Italy, Emilio Salgari; in Germany, Charles Seals-field, Friedrich Gerstäcker, and Balduin Möllhausen. All were prolific writers (Balduin Möllhausen wrote more than 150 books and most of the others as many as thirty), and all were translated widely. Their school of literature (if it may be thus called) was climaxed at the end of the century when Karl May introduced the ultimate *Westmann,* Old Shatter-hand, and his faithful Indian companion, Winnetou, to the German public. May's seventy novels have sold thirty million copies in over twenty languages, and still sell a million copies yearly. An annual Karl May Festival in West Germany attracts some 150,000 of the dedicated; Karl May films, and Karl May plays, and Karl May toys have captivated, and still captivate, a sizeable portion of Europe's population.

The American West pictured by these sensation ped-dlers was an unbelievable fantasy land where savage animals and equally savage Indians lurked in tropical forests, where fights with daggers and revolvers were part of the daily routine, and where life was of uncertain duration for all not prepared to kill an opponent before he could whip his bowie knife from its sheath or his forty-five from its holster. Certainly this Wild West bore not the faintest resemblance to the West that was: a West of sweating farmers, cowboys who more often worked in derby hats than sombreros (and

many of whom were Negroes or Mexican Americans), and law-abiding citizens whose principal objective was to reproduce the orderly societies of the East as rapidly as possible. Why this distortion?

Ignorance was not always the answer. Karl May did not visit the United States until just before his death, but other novelists knew the frontier well; Charles Sealsfield lived for years in the Southwest, much of Gustave Aimard's youth was spent beyond the Mississippi, and Balduin Möllhausen gained his first fame accompanying exploring expeditions into the Rocky Mountain country. Yet truth cramped their writing but slightly. Instead their imaginative creations were molded to the tastes of their sensation-seeking audiences, who then, as now, thirsted for vicarious thrills. A Texan visiting in London during the 1840s realized this when he met some of England's most eminent intellectuals. "They listened with deference to all that I said," he reported, "but . . . with delight to the accounts of our Indian fights, Prairie life, and buffalo hunts." The temptation to cater to the whims of readers demanding ever more excitement was too profitable to be resisted.

Some of the exaggerations of novelists and travelers can be forgiven as typical—and delightful—tall tales. No reader could possibly believe that the soil in Arkansas was so rich that settlers made candles by dipping wicks in mud puddles, or that land in Kansas was so fertile that it produced fifty bushels of maize to the acre when none had been planted. Nor could the most gullible take seriously the account of a buffalo hunt in which an Indian was caught in the middle of a stampeding herd but escaped by leaping from back to back of the charging beasts, pausing in his flight to lance some of the fattest cows.

But less excusable were fantasies only slightly less unbelievable: the Gila River Valley (actually an arid desert) teeming with alligators, monstrous boa constrictors, and giant basilisks "crawling silent and sinister beneath the leaves"; an Apache heroine, White Gazelle, dressed in "loose

Turkish trowsers, made of Indian cashmere, fastened at the knees with diamond garters . . . while a jacket of violet velvet, buttoned over the bosom with a profusion of diamonds, displayed her exquisite bust;" an earthquake that sloshed the Colorado River over its banks to quench a forest fire that threatened the hero; an ostrich hunt staged by the Blackfeet Indians of Montana that ended with a great feast "for the ostrich is excellent eating, and the Indians prepare, chiefly from the meat on the breast, a dish renowned for its delicacy and exquisite flavor."

Novelists and travelers paid only slightly more tribute to actuality when they described the frontiersmen who peopled these wilds. Three types were identified: *hunters,* who roamed far ahead of the settlements; *squatters,* who made the first assault on the wilderness; and *pioneers,* who extended their clearings and heralded the first coming of civilization. Actually there was little to distinguish these stereotypes; all three represented stages in the degradation of civilized man. Yet the image-makers elevated the hunter, who was actually the least savory of the lot, to a role as hero, picturing him as a godlike superman ennobled spiritually by daily contacts with nature. Conversely they painted the squatters as barbarous social outcasts, and the pioneers as not much better—crude, unmannerly illiterates unworthy of the company of cultured men.

These distinctions, both false and artificial as they were, demonstrate the persistence of traditionalism in myth making. The *hunter* was a type long familiar to readers and hence demanded by them—a reincarnation of the "Child of Nature" so glorified in eighteenth century romanticism. Reared in the forests' haunting silence, these "primitive-strong" (as a German writer named them) blended the best of primitivism and civilization. Cruel they were, for they must kill the Indians who blocked their countrymen's path westward, but their cruelty was transcended by an inner nobility. This was God-given, the gift of intimacy with the Creator through His creations. "Among them," wrote a Ger-

man novelist, "I have observed a genius which would have done honor to the greatest philosophers of ancient and modern times." He was speaking, mind you, of semibarbarians, most of them illiterate, who had traded civilization's restraints for savagery's brutal freedom.

The *squatters,* by contrast, were depicted as near animals who had rejected civilization without acquiring any of nature's blessings. "The very outcasts of society," they were called; "the scum and the dregs." Sunk in sloth and laziness, they were destined to flee forever from normal humans. The *pioneers* were little better. They were pictured as crude, boastful, ill-mannered braggarts, living slovenly lives, and disdainful of the higher values that distinguished civilized men from barbarians.

Image-makers delighted in isolating traits of the pioneers that they found especially annoying. One was their eternal boasting. Travelers reported listening to an incessant litany of self-praise: "The Americans were *more* learned, *more* powerful, and altogether *more* extraordinary than any other people in the world." The United States had the most fertile soils, the strongest armies, the biggest cities, the largest rivers, the noisiest thunder, and (according to one traveler) the longest history of any nation on the globe. Conversely the rest of the world was a decaying ruin. Asia was a heathen backwash doomed to perpetual misrule; Europe was sunk in despotism and poverty—"A heap of medieval feudal states . . . that have not enough vitality to rise from the abyss of misery and corruption into which they have fallen as a result of centuries of ignorance and despotism." The New World was outstripping the Old; soon England would be known only as the mother of the United States.

Just as annoying as the constant "puffing" (to use the language of the day) were the abominable manners of the "squatters" and "pioneers." Their principal offense against good taste was their constant tobacco chewing. Along the frontiers, said the image-makers, all men's jaws were perpetually in motion as they chewed and spit, chewed and

spit, for all the world (to quote a Polish observer) "as though they were some species of ruminating animal." The entire West, indoors and out, was carpeted with dried tobacco juice, while spitters were a constant menace even though most were good shots; "when you are surrounded with shooters," as one traveler wrote feelingly, "you feel nervous." So universal was the habit that the twang noticeable in western speech was ascribed to the fact that westerners' mouths were always so full of juice that they could not be opened without overflowing, forcing the pioneers to speak through their noses.

Above all, the frontier was a Babylon of Barbarism. On the Mississippi Valley frontier rough-and-tumble fights occurred daily, with each battler striving to bite off the nose, claw off the ears, or gouge out the eyes of his opponent. Eye gouging particularly lent itself to gory descriptions; travelers devoted page after page to imaginary battles that ended with one fighter plunging his thumbs into an enemy's eye, or rising from the fray with the symbol of victory —his opponent's eyeball—held in his hand. West of the Mississippi lethal battles with bowie knives and six-shooters became the stock-in-trade of the image-makers, for in that Wild West of their creation every man was armed and the code of honor demanded instant retaliation for every insult, real or imagined. An English visitor, inquiring whether a revolver was necessary, was told: "Well, you mout not need one for a month, and you mout not need one for three months, but ef you ever did want one, you kin bet you'll want it mighty sudden." Legal justice was totally lacking in this make-believe land.

The image projected by novelists and travelers—of crude, ill-mannered frontiersmen and a lawless society—was a forbidding one, and hence hardly pleasing to another group of image-makers. These were promoters whose purpose was to attract immigrants to the West: guidebook authors, agents for land-grant railroads eager to sell their excess holdings, propagandists for land and immigration com-

panies, and particularly successful immigrants hoping to lure their former countrymen to the land they found so rewarding. The immigrant letters home—the "America Letters" as they are called—were particularly effective, for they were believed to be utterly trustworthy. "America Letters" spanned the oceans by the thousands during the nineteenth century, were read in village churches, published in local newspapers, and played a major role in picturing frontier life to the rest of the world.

The image that they projected differed so markedly from that of novelists and travelers that those who read were forced to make a difficult decision. Should they believe that the frontier was a brutalizing wasteland, or a new Canaan assuring prosperity and freedom to all? Faced with this dilemma, some simply rejected what they disliked hearing; others accepted both images as valid, but ranked one above the other on their own value scale. A Norwegian folk ballad pictured a would-be emigrant as he pondered this decision:

> I know the venture will cost me dear in the hardships of exposure to sun and storm, in fierce battles with scorpions and serpents and wild beasts, in deadly duels with drawn daggers. But that is better than to fight one's own people and get nothing for it.

That millions of Europeans and Asians decided to migrate testified to that effectiveness of the image-makers who sang of the American West as a land of promise.

And what a promising land they pictured. A farm of one's own—an impossibility in most of the world—was assured all. A penniless immigrant could hire out as a farm worker at a dollar a day, for there was work for all in the labor-hungry West. He could live on two dollars a week, saving enough each fortnight to purchase ten acres of land so fertile that it had only to be scratched to produce abundant crops. With a farm of his own he was assured perpetual freedom from want or care. On the frontier all ate meat three times a day, and wood was so plentiful that cabins

were never cold. More food was thrown to the dogs in a week in a frontier home than a European peasant consumed in a year. Imagine the longings of a German who seldom tasted meat reading of a frontiersman in a western inn filling his plate twice with beef, pork, venison, chicken, turkey, and fish, then ordering a large bowl of soup because "soup trickles down . . . where beef and ham try in vain to enter." He might agree with an Irish slogan: "The only place in Ireland where a man can make a fortune is America."

Such exaggerations might be questioned, but who could doubt the testimony of former neighbors when their "America Letters" recited their success stories in simple prose: "We sold our farm last winter for $800"; "We have five horses, seventeen cattle, thirteen sheep, and twenty-four hogs"; "I have deposited $800 in the bank"; "Our farm is worth five or six thousand dollars"; "I have 140 acres of land fenced, and nearly 30 under a good state of improvement." "After five or six years," a Japanese guidebook promised, "the person having no pennies will become a very rich man."

The universality of this image of frontier prosperity was attested by ballad-makers who carried the promises of the image-makers into the realm of absurdity. In the West of their creation lay a new Eden where "the hedges consist of sides of bacon and tobacco, so that you may lie in the shade of the bacon and smoke the tobacco"; where "tea and coffee and clotted cream fairly drown the settlers, pork and wheat are one's daily bread, and everyone lolls on the lap of fortune." Throughout Scandinavia peasants sang—and still sing—the interminable verses of "Oleana":

> They give you land for nothing in jolly Oleana
> And grain comes leaping from the ground in floods of
>     golden manna.
> The grain it does the threshing, it pours into the sack, Sir,
> So you can take a quiet nap, a-stretching on your back, Sir.

> The little roasted piggies, with manners quite demure, Sir,
> They ask, "Will you have some?" and then you say, "Why
>   sure, Sir."

To reach that land of promise was the "collective utopian dream" of thousands.

Particularly when the frontier offered something even more alluring than abundance: the promise of equality and freedom. If any phrase appeared more often in "America Letters" than "We eat meat three times a day," it was "Here we tip our hats to no one." In a new land where men were few and necessary tasks many, all who worked were respected, no matter how menial their duties. The manual laborer contributed to society no less than the merchant or lawyer, and deserved to be treated in the same way. "Here," wrote a recent immigrant, "workingmen are not afraid of their masters; they are seen as equals."

Such class distinctions as did exist, all agreed, were based on wealth rather than lineage. What a man was, not what his family had been, determined his place in society. "Out West," a British visitor reported, "the one question asked is 'What can you do?' not 'Who was your father?' " Another who mentioned ancestors to a frontiersman was told: "We don't vally those things in this country; it's what's above ground, not what's under, that we think on." Given these standards, a place in the upper crust of society awaited all who were enterprising. Gentlemen could be made of the coarsest stuff where a fortunate speculation could overnight transform the village pauper into the community's richest—and hence most respected—citizen. "In Europe," Germans were told, "a man works to live; here he works to become rich."

With equality went liberty—the liberty to think and act as one chose. "Here," a recent arrival wrote his old neighbors, "no emperor and no king has the right to command us to do anything." Where all were equal, all governed; a common citizen had the right to slander and damn his government, abuse public officials to their faces, and call the

President of the United States a fool without calling down the wrath of his fellows or the firm hand of the law. "Here I am free," was a repeated phrase in "America Letters."

Personal independence was so venerated that it was sometimes asserted in extreme form. A traveler who objected to the off-key singing of a boatman was told that "he was in a land of liberty," and had no right to interfere. A lad on the Illinois frontier, scolded by his mother for appropriating a piece of cake, answered: "Why, Mother, aren't we in a free country now?" Another, ordered by his father to fetch some wood, was heard to say: "Go get it yourself, you old son of a bitch." The father turned to the witness, his face aglow with satisfaction. "A sturdy republican, sir," he said. Absurdities, perhaps, but they mirrored the outlawing of subserviency on the frontier.

Such were the mores of republicanism reported by image-makers that any social distinctions were vigorously opposed by frontiersmen. This seemed logical; in a land where abundance was within the reach of the most humble, there could be no humble. Travelers soon learned that they risked insult, if not injury, if they forgot that simple fact. One titled Englishman, hunting in Colorado, asked his guide to fill the tub in which he bathed. The guide suggested that he take a swim in the Platte River, then exploded: "You ain't quite the top-shelfer you think you is. You ain't even got a shower-bath for cooling your swelled head. But I'll make you a present of one, boss!" And, pulling his revolver, he shot the tub full of holes. Often told were tales of the traveler who sent for a tailor to be measured for a coat and was told that such a procedure was not republican, of the serving maid who refused to allow her mistress to ring for her unless she could ring for the mistress whenever "she desired to have speech with her," of the hostler requested to call a guest in the morning shouting, "Call yourself and be damned."

Titles were taboo in that egalitarian society. All men

were Mr. and referred to each other as gentlemen; all women were Madam or Miss and were universally called ladies. Travelers from less democratic lands never tired of listing examples of frontier usage: the coachman who asked his passenger, "Are you the man going to Portland because if you are, I'm the gentleman that's going to drive you"; the frontier landlord who asked a group of stagecoach drivers, "Which is the gentleman who brought this man here?"; the court defendant who testified that "he and another gentleman had been shoveling mud"; the newspaper report of "two gentlemen who were convicted and sentenced to six months' imprisonment for horse stealing."

Personal relationships were as democratized as forms of address, according to the image-makers. This was particularly true in frontier inns where laborers and judges, drovers and merchants, magistrates and stagecoach drivers, dined side by side, waited on by "helps" (the word *servant* was never used) who addressed them by their first names, leaned over chairs to take part in the conversation, and shed their coats to join in a game of cards when the meal was over. This was offensive enough to class-conscious visitors, but worse was the application of democratic principles to sleeping arrangements. Guests were assigned to beds in the order of their arrival, with two, three, or four in each bed. Judges snored next to teamsters, legislators beside wagoners, bankers with hog drivers as their partners. "A most almighty beautiful democratic amalgam" one westerner was heard to call it. But hardly pleasing to the fastidious, for guests were changed more often than the sheets. One who objected was rudely reminded that "since *gentlemen* are all alike, people do not see why they should not sleep in the same sheets."

The image-makers who pictured the American frontier for their readers performed their task well. By the 1890s, wrote a Czech publicist, "the most illiterate peasant in the Balkans, who did not even know the name of his county-

seat, knew about America, about its free land and the absence of landlords." That peasant knew, as did others throughout much of the world, that the American West was a land of abundance and opportunity, of equality and freedom, where land was assured the industrious and where the upper ranks of society were open to the humble. "A nation of sovereigns," an Irish newspaper called it with some reason.

The projection of this image played a role, no matter how minor, in stirring the spirit of rebellion that underlay many of the economic, social, and political reforms of the late nineteenth and early twentieth centuries. Peasant farmers in Europe who learned of a land where all ate meat three times daily and tipped their hats to no one would no longer accept their subservient role with the same docile humility. Their horizons had been widened, their ambitions stirred by visions of a better life. "This people," wrote a Swedish publicist, "which has for so many years been satisfied with its meager lot, has begun to reason with itself, and has found that things could be better than they are." The seeds of discontent had been planted, and only domestic reforms could keep them in check.

These remade many of the Old World's institutions, but nowhere did the frontier image play a more important role than in the debate over the right of men—all men—to govern themselves. Liberals and conservatives agreed that the lot of the poor in the American West was better than in the Old World. They disagreed on why. Liberals, favoring reform, insisted that the higher living standards there were the product of domestic institutions; the frontier was a paradise for small farmers because small farmers shaped its policies. Liberalize government in the Old World, they said, and it will reward the liberalizers by the same affluence enjoyed by the New.

Conservatives answered that American prosperity and equality were the products solely of cheap western lands

and hence beyond the grasp of settled nations. Manhood suffrage succeeded simply because the frontier drained workers from the East, thus intensifying competition for jobs and elevating the wages of those who remained, at the same time syphoning off the discontented who posed the greatest threat to the social system. Cheap lands also equalized the ownership of property, allowing the majority a stake in society, and with it the sense of social responsibility necessary for a stable electorate. Older nations, with no reservoir of occupiable land, were unsuited to democracy. Wrote the editor of England's *Quarterly Review:* "The inexhaustible fund of unoccupied land . . . exempts the great body of the lower classes from what in other countries is the most usual and fruitful source of popular discontent and tumult, namely, the pressure of want."

The effectiveness of this argument was demonstrated by reformers in Denmark, Sweden, Norway, and Prussia when they acknowledged the validity of the frontier as a "safety-valve" by trying to create artificial frontiers to drain away excess workers and raise the living standards of the remainder. In Denmark this ambition helps explain the *Husmand* Movement designed to parcel great estates among small holders; in Norway and Sweden it underlay an effort to drain swamp lands and open hitherto unoccupied northern territories to peasants; in Prussia it was directed toward dividing the giant Junker holdings. These moves failed, but their popularity suggests that the image of the American frontier as a land of promise was not lost on social critics in older countries.

No one would suggest that the frontier image was solely or even largely responsible for the social, economic, and political changes that altered Old World institutions during the dawning years of the present century. Yet there seems little question that that image bred discontent among the least advantaged classes in Europe (and to a lesser degree in Asia), and helped set in motion the alterations that

eventually bettered their lot. The image-makers, whether exuberant guidebook writers, land promoters, imaginative novelists, travelers, or the homespun authors of "America Letters," helped shape the course of history, and deserve a larger place in its annals than they have been accorded.

# IN DEFENSE OF LIBERTY:
## EXTREMISM AND OTHER VICES [3]

### JUDITH F. KRUG [4]

In 1974 a controversy arose in Kanawha County, West Virginia (near Charleston), over whether certain textbooks used in the Charleston public schools were "antireligious, Communistic and pornographic." Peaceful picketing soon deteriorated into the bombing of three schools, setting automobiles afire, and sympathetic strikes at nearby coal mines. The protest in West Virginia was not an isolated case. Conservative parents harassed school officials in East Baton Rouge parish, where Louisiana State University is located. To the librarians and the university community, book burning, censorship, interference in the operation of the schools, and witch hunts are extremely distasteful. Hence, the lecture committee of the LSU library decided to invite to the campus Judith F. Krug, director of the Office for Intellectual Freedom of the American Library Association. This choice was fortunate because she had "participated as the American Library Association's representative in the National Education Association's inquiry into the Kanawha County textbook controversy." In other words, she was able to discuss the problem from first-hand observation. On April 17, 1975, she delivered an address entitled "In Defense of Liberty: Extremism and Other Vices," in the Library Lecture Series, at the Colonnade in the LSU Student Union to an audience of 175 to 200 librarians, faculty members, students, and other interested citizens. She was introduced by Dr. Charles Patterson, associate professor in the Graduate School of Library Science.

The lecture was most timely, for on the very day of the lecture the East Baton Rouge Parish School Board met with a group of protesting parents involved in the issue of censorship of certain textbooks. As a result Judith Krug was interviewed over two local television stations and was consulted by members of the school staff.

[3] Delivered as the 32nd in the LSU Library Lecture Series, at the Union Colonnade, Louisiana State University, Baton Rouge, 2:00 P.M. April 17, 1975. The series is supported by a grant from Mrs. Ella V. Aldrich Schwing. Quoted by permission.

[4] For biographical note, see Appendix.

Krug proved to be an animated and convincing speaker who generated enthusiasm among her listeners. When she finished her formal presentation, several listeners asked her questions and made further comments about intellectual freedom.

The lecture was particularly significant because the speaker placed the textbook controversy in a larger context and showed from diverse points of view how fundamental beliefs in freedom of information were violated. Krug strove to separate rationality from emotionalism. Further, she suggested that conflict over the grade school textbooks was a sign of anxiety among parents over losing control of their local schools and also a sign of "latent institutionalized racism." Behind the attacks she saw "highly sophisticated, well-financed, and extremely arrogant groups."

"It shows what a poor job our schools have done in the past if so many people feel that the free exchange of opinion is communism and the total absence of debate is 'freedom.' " A teacher from Kanawha County, West Virginia, made that statement. And it seems to me to exemplify where we stand today in our battle to preserve the concept of intellectual freedom.

Since this essay is devoted to intellectual freedom, I should first define my use of the term. In its pure sense, the concept embodies the right of any person to believe what he wants on any subject, and to express his beliefs orally or graphically, publicly or privately, as he deems appropriate. The ability to express opinions, however, does not mean very much if there is not someone on the receiving end to hear what one is saying or read what one has written. And so intellectual freedom has a second part: total and complete freedom of access to all information and ideas, regardless of the media of communication used. This, in turn, gives each person the basis on which to form his own opinions and decisions. Once these are formed, he, too, is free to express his beliefs. Intellectual freedom, then, is a circle —a circle broken if either the ability to produce or access to the productions is stifled.

As I use the term, *intellectual freedom* means not only the ability of creators to express themselves through what-

ever media they choose, but also *access* to their creations—access by all persons, regardless of their age, race, sex, religion, national origin, or social or political points of view.

The concept derives from the First Amendment and is fundamental to our constitutional republican form of government. And because it is primary, the strong and sustained attack now being made on it—in the name of liberty and freedom—is all the more frightening.

Where did it all start? How did our opinions and our beliefs, even our language, become so twisted? I can't answer those questions, of course. I might point out that the seeds of conservatism are an integral part of the fabric of American society, and that these seeds have played a great role in the development of our country and our society—more so than their number would seem to warrant. But as we approach our two hundredth birthday, the seeds seem to be flowering.

After a decade of nourishment composed of assassinations, riots, Vietnam, Watergate, a runaway economy, depression, unemployment, a general attack on authority, the flowers springing forth intertwine to form an oppressive blanket of pervasive anti-intellectualism. In my opinion, this anti-intellectualism presents to the concept of intellectual freedom its greatest challenge since the days of Joe McCarthy. Anti-intellectualism, as defined by Richard Hofstadter is "A resentment and suspicion of the life of the mind and of those who are considered to represent it; and a disposition constantly to minimize the value of that life."

Now, no matter how you turn it, intellectual freedom concerns itself with the life of the mind. Indeed, the concept—in its physical representations (materials)—provides the food from which the mind nourishes its life. And we need look only as far as Kanawha County, West Virginia, to see a manifestation of the resentment and suspicion to which Hofstadter refers.

The textbook controversy which spawned in that West Virginia community concerned the adoption of elementary language arts textbooks, involving more than three hundred separate materials from several publishers. The controversy is possibly the most violent outburst over textbooks that has ever occurred in the history of American education. And it is the extremes to which the elements in the controversy were carried that make it unique—not the elements, themselves, which composed it.

Many people have wondered just what horrendous things elementary "language arts" readers could have in them to have created so much havoc. It's rather hard to explain to these people that the books are merely collections of poems, essays, stories, and the like. They're not particularly special and even the fact that a few stories contain profanity—which a lot of the people objected to—did not make the books very different from what you find in almost any magazine on the newsstand today. In fact, the particular books could easily have been replaced by others.

Having participated as the American Library Association's representative in the National Education Association's inquiry into the Kanawha County textbook controversy, I have come to believe that the textbooks weren't really the reason for the fight in Charleston. They were, instead, the excuse. I say this because, during the course of its investigation, the panel questioned not only textbook supporters, but a large number of the protesters—and when we asked the average Kanawha County resident to what they objected in the books, they couldn't tell us. They did hand out mimeographed pages from a sex education handbook—but that handbook was not even in circulation in Charleston schools. In fact, one of the most nefarious pieces of propaganda circulated by the protesters contained quotes from a *high school* textbook that was not even on the list of the materials being protested against and the quotes were sandwiched between reproductions from a sex educa-

tion manual, of which there was one copy in the entire county—in the public library!

The panel was told about stories supposedly contained in the books, but which subsequent research showed didn't even exist. There was one about "the man who chokes a girl to death." It turned out to be a story about a doctor who forces a frightened little girl to open her mouth so he can save her life.

Well, then, if the fight wasn't really over the textbooks— what was it all about? It was about fear, it was about frustration, it was about helplessness and powerlessness. It was about a county that physically covers 940 square miles, miles encompassing a sophisticated metropolitan area (Charleston) and the creeks and hollows of the southern end of what is known as Appalachia. It was about the power-brokers residing in Charleston and the "hillbillies" who people the creeks and hollows. Yet, the hillbillies were not as you might see them in your stereotyped image. Excellent transportation and communication—good roads, television and telephone—have brought the twentieth century to this region. But while modern conveniences have brought the twentieth century in some aspects, it has not infringed upon the religion—which is fundamentalist. And so the controversy was also about "people who believe in books and people who believe in The Book."

The controversy was about the West Virginia education laws, laws that mandate that each county will have only one school district; laws that stipulate state adoption of books for the elementary grades; and laws that decree that the materials used as basic texts within the school districts be multicultural and multiethnic.

The controversy was also about the loss of parental control over the local schools, due to consolidation—or so the protesters believed. "Consolidation," which became a rallying point for the protesters, referred to the closing of the one- and two-room schoolhouses that were previously sit-

uated within the various local population groupings. Many children in the creeks and hollows are now bused as much as thirty miles each way each day. Removal of the site of education from within the community increased the parents' feelings of helplessness and isolation, for they no longer could easily check on what their kids were doing in school. They no longer could see who was teaching their children, and they no longer could easily voice their protests against what they considered blasphemous "Commie" ideas. Interestingly, the people spoke of consolidation as if it happened yesterday—when in truth it began approximately forty years ago, in 1935!

The controversy was about the parents' belief that their children are not learning: newer textbooks introduced into the Kanawha County classrooms are not only multicultural and multiethnic—but reflect modern, progressive theories of education. No longer are the three Rs set out at specific times of the day and as subjects within themselves. Rather, traditional subjects are contained as strands running throughout, in this case, the English curriculum.

Multiethnic, multicultural texts, however, are not unique to Kanawha County—nor indeed, to West Virginia. In fact, the reduction of cultural and rural isolation of American children have been objectives openly promulgated by the United States Congress and the United States Office of Education. Indeed, large amounts of federal funds are directly connected to the willingness of all the states and all the school districts to adopt materials which help to reduce such cultural isolation. In Kanawha County, however, the "new" textbooks, encompassing as they do a new philosophy of education and a new method of instruction, gave a dissatisfied people a handle on which to hang a protest. It is a protest that brought prolonged civil strife and uncivil conduct, pitting neighbor against neighbor, church against church, the school system against segments of the community, provoking discord among the teachers themselves, and doing violence to the education of students. The contro-

versy raised questions about the basic nature, purpose, and changing methods of public education, and the rights of the various groups involved in it—parents, students, educators and school boards—to determine the content of educational programming.

The controversy also brought to the surface a latent, institutionalized racism and provided for certain extremist groups, a means by which to further their own programs. And finally, the Kanawha County textbook controversy provided the most visible example to date of the anti-intellectualism pervading the country.

This anti-intellectualism is one of Richard Nixon's legacies. That it is directed toward education and the educated is another. We cannot be surprised at such legacies—not from a man who dismissed the protections of the Bill of Rights as anachronistic, and confessed that he had no confidence in the virtue or in the intelligence of the American people, or, for that matter, in their representatives in Congress. It was because of this latter belief (or maybe the belief was the justification of the action) that he chose to conceal his own activities, foreign and domestic alike, in a fog of secrecy. And now that the fog is lifting, the gulf between our professed beliefs and reality is more than most Americans can assimilate.

The result is a dismay, a bewilderment, about what has happened to "America." Life is so complex today that most people have absolutely no hope of controlling what happens around them and to them—and even more important, most people can't even understand what's happening.

The people do know that there is a problem—and in the true American tradition, "if there's a problem, we'll solve it." We'll solve it even if it can't be identified or understood. And one obvious solution is to reform the schools and the libraries—those great big edifices that take so much of our tax money and to thank us, they plant revolutionary ideas in our kids' minds. Reform begins by reinstituting local control and after this is accomplished, it is easy to re-

turn to the teaching of "traditional" principles and values. To quote one of the dissidents from Kanawha County, "we must go back to those principles which made America great and kept it that way for two hundred years."

Unfortunately, going back to those traditional principles and values must, by the very nature of the protesters' demands, erase every civil and human right that has been won in the last twenty-five years: the right of racial and ethnic minority groups to be included in the textbooks; the right of all students to learn that in the world and in this society, white is not always right; that white, middle-class values are not the only, nor even always the best, values; and that the history of the United States is not one long, unblemished record of Christian benevolence and virtue.

Of course, there's no denying that going back to the "traditional" values of America not only makes life easier, but certainly more understandable. Those were the good old days when free enterprise held sway and the end justified any means—sweatshops, slave wages, child labor, stepping on anyone who got in your way as you progressed up the ladder to wealth and security; the days when George Washington didn't tell a lie at all, and when he was sleeping around—by golly, he really was sleeping.

In this movement backward—in the drive to return to a less complex, more understandable era—much help, unfortunately, is available. It's unfortunate because the "help" is exacerbating the anti-intellectualism. In the last few months, the demands have been growing to remove materials from classrooms and school libraries that first, do not meet "community standards" and second, that undermine the family as the basic societal unit.

The first demand can be traced directly to a *mis*interpretation of the Supreme Court's First Amendment decisions of June 1973 and June 1974; a misinterpretation promulgated, particularly, by Citizens for Decency Through Law. CDL, which contends that it is not an organization devoted to censorship, but rather one which is anxious to

help the citizens uphold the law of the land, appears wherever the forces of darkness seem to be faltering—before state legislatures considering new legislation affecting the right to read, at rallies protesting textbooks and library materials, before church groups anxious to find means by which to regain their wandering flocks. CDL's national spokesman was in Kanawha County, West Virginia, for seven weeks. When I asked this man if his presence in Kanawha County meant that CDL was against the textbooks, he said, "No, we are not." The next logical question—and my next question—was, "Well, then, what were you doing there?" He did not respond—but one of the Kanawha County protesters did. I was informed that "Bob" was there advising them on the kinds of activities they could undertake and statements they could make in order to reach their goal of removing all of the protested books from the Kanawha County school system. After all, I was told, the Supreme Court said that each local community could determine what kind of materials they wanted.

That, of course, was not exactly what the Supreme Court had said. Indeed, in overturning the decisions of the lower courts in the *Carnal Knowledge* case, the Supreme Court specifically said that local standards did not permit the particular community "unbridled discretion" in determining what could be banned.

And yet, censorship is an easy solution to complex—if not insoluble—problems. There are people who believe that if children are not permitted to read books related to drugs, books like *Go Ask Alice,* the drug problem will disappear. There are people who believe that reading Eldridge Cleaver's *Soul on Ice* results in "rape, illegitimacy, abortion, sex perversion, and venereal disease." (Concerned Citizens Committee of Greenwich, Connecticut) There are people who believe that banning *Boss* by Mike Royko will simultaneously ban machine politics; others who believe that *Catcher in the Rye* is responsible for children's disrespect for their parents, if not all adults. And there are actually

people who believe that textbook content flows linearly and uninterruptedly from the printed page into the student's mind, causing an immediate change in behavior; that textbook content is always absorbed, and never forgotten; that the teacher agrees with everything in the textbook and teaches it literally; that children in school learn in isolation, never influenced by their peers and never testing what the textbook says against their own experience; and finally, that textbooks and learning are synonymous.

And to all these people censorship by community standards is the solution. It's a simplistic solution, but it's easily attainable and very real to those who will accept it.

Thanks to the misinterpretation of the Supreme Court guidelines, a school administrator in Hartford, Michigan, during a recent controversy over *Each Other's Victims,* by Milton Travers, could recommend a community referendum as the means to preclude future problems. What he meant was that every book that was adopted for the school curriculum—and every book that was selected for the school libraries—should be placed before the community for its vote. The majority, in every case, would carry the day.

And it's not only school administrators who see community standards as the final solution. Recently, the mayor of Covina, California, suggested that residents should be allowed to vote in their own communities "to determine if we want to consider some people legitimate businessmen." What raised his ire was a bookstore which was not X-rated but carried materials he considered salacious. The mayor went on to say that "there is no way the county can succeed unless we can protect the rights of the majority." If I remember correctly, however, the Bill of Rights guarantees the rights of the minority. For if minority rights are lost, if the First Amendment founders, we have indeed lost the matrix of our freedoms.

Utilizing "community standards" to determine the availability of materials is only one part of the attack. The second part can be traced to the dismay and bewilderment—

even fear—of the citizenry in general; it is a fear around which many extremist groups are focusing programs. One example is the new Conservative Caucus, which includes in its platform, a plank entitled The Right to Educational Freedom. As an explanation, the Conservative Caucus states:

The right of parents to define the conditions and content of their children's education must outweigh the power of government to interfere in the selection of textbooks or teachers, or to use the schools to advance the political, cultural and social objectives of government officials. There must be *no forced busing.*

Another relatively new group is the Heritage Foundation, which "pledges itself to the pursuit and dissemination of truth as it is embodied in the Constitution of the United States and the free market economic principles on which the Constitution is predicated."

A final example is the John Birch Society's Project of the Month, for February 1975. The Birch project urged all members to do their part to reestablish the family as the basic societal unit and to reassert parental authority, by undertaking, among other activities, a careful review of the materials that children are "forced" to use in the classroom and the school library.

Ironically, it was a Kanawha County resident who brought the Birch project to our attention. She had called the Office for Intellectual Freedom seeking help to counter an attack on school libraries by the same Board of Education member who gained notoriety in the textbook controversy. The books targeted for immediate removal included *The Naked Ape, Soul on Ice,* and *The Cheerleader* by Ruth Doan McDougal. Having removed the offending books, the next step in the project was to develop guidelines. These guidelines would rid libraries of those materials that undermine "traditional principles and values" and would also ensure that such revolutionary ideas never again found their way into the libraries of the Kanawha County school system.

Guidelines are not new to Kanawha County, for in No-

vember 1974 the Board adopted a set of guidelines for textbook selection. Among these guidelines is one that states: "Textbooks for use in the classrooms of Kanawha County shall recognize the sanctity of the home and emphasize its importance as the basic unit of American society." Another guideline states: "Textbooks must not intrude into the privacy of students' homes by asking personal questions about the inner feelings or behavior of themselves or their parents by direct question, statement or inference." As envisioned by the promulgator of these guidelines, they mean that a teacher may no longer ask a student, "How do you feel about that," or "What do you think about this?" Another guideline directs: "Textbooks shall teach the true history and heritage of the United States. . . ." And to that I must ask—just who is to determine the *true* history and heritage?

I should point out that just as the guidelines are not unique to Kanawha County, neither was that telephone call an isolated incident. You need only look at recent issues of the ALA's *Newsletter on Intellectual Freedom* to see how very much the pressures have escalated in just the past eight months.

Who loses in these incidents? Certainly, the children. But just as importantly, every such incident, every project, every misinterpretation erodes—however slightly—the bedrock of the constitutional republic. Censorship is anathema to the United States of America. And censorship occurs when just one human being is precluded from making known his ideas to another human being. The situation has reached crisis proportions when a school district in the United States mandates the selection of textbooks that contain the truth and by virtue of the mandate indicate that those who have passed it, indeed, know the truth. It is incredible to me that we have not learned over the past two hundred years—and particularly the last two years—that the First Amendment is indivisible, that it is indeed the matrix of all our freedoms and the bedrock of the constitutional

republic. What the protesters in Kanawha County—and all would-be censors throughout the United States—seem to have forgotten is that the constitutional republican form of government is only as effective as its electorate is enlightened. If we are going to have government by the people, for the people, and of the people—the people must have information available to them on which to form their decisions, their opinions, and their actions.

Sadly, the threats facing the concept of intellectual freedom today are not the kind of threats to which we've become accustomed. We are not currently dealing with well-meaning individuals—but rather with highly sophisticated, well-financed, and extremely arrogant groups. These groups are manipulating the citizenry by playing on the fears that a complex and uncontrollable society have raised. And they are focusing on the soft underbelly of the republic, for they are attacking the school system and through the school system our children to whom the torch of liberty must eventually pass. And if the children are not permitted to develop their abilities to think, to discern truth from falsehood, to perceive right from wrong while they are growing up—then the quest for a quality education is meaningless and the constitutional republic must fail.

And yet I do not believe that the republic must fail, for once recognizing that there is a problem, we can formulate the issues and seek means to combat them. Indeed, we might look on the current situation as a golden opportunity. We may finally have reached the time where the outlook for intellectual freedom is so bad that it couldn't be better. Perhaps our time has come—for the library remains the only public institution in the United States where materials representing all points of view are available. The library does not require attendance, nor any particular point of view, nor required reading, nor even acceptance. It does provide a pool of information covering the spectrum of social and political thought from which each individual, according to his own needs, wants, and intellectual development, can

choose what he wishes. The library is still the one and only place where the dictates of the First Amendment can be fulfilled.

Article III of the *Library Bill of Rights* says, "Censorship should be challenged by libraries in the maintenance of their responsibility to provide public information and enlightenment." While our record is respectable, even the library profession has not challenged every instance of censorship. And of those we have challenged, we surely have not been uniformly successful. Yet, winning or losing seems to me to be less important than continuing to bring censorship, in all its guises and disguises, to the public's attention.

And as we strive to fulfill our responsibilities, we can take heart and draw sustenance from the words of James Madison, which still ring true 150 years after they were written:

A popular government, without popular information, or the means of acquiring it, is but a prologue to a farce or a tragedy; or perhaps both. Knowledge will forever govern ignorance; and a people who mean to be their own governors, must arm themselves with the power which knowledge gives.

# A HERO HONORED

## A WARRIOR AGAINST FATE [1]

### Dudley T. Cornish [2]

Wishing to memorialize the heroism of a native son who gave his life for his country, the citizens of Pittsburg, Kansas, dedicated their new United States Army Reserve Training Center to Second Lieutenant William M. Benefield Jr. This young black soldier, who died in action in the Korean conflict on July 29, 1950, had graduated from Pittsburg High School and attended Kansas State College of Pittsburg. The memorial ceremony took place on Sunday afternoon, November 16, before a large audience of local citizens, members of the Reserve Unit, and the members of the Benefield family, greatly respected in the city.

The speaker, Dr. Dudley T. Cornish, chairman of the department of history at Kansas State College of Pittsburg, was a wise choice. He knew the family personally and the officers of the Center, many of whom were his former students. Long interested in black history, he had written *The Sable Arm: Negro Troops in the Union Army, 1861-1865* (Norton, 1966) and had served in World War II, moving from the rank of private to that of captain.

The eloquence of the speech emerges from the way the speaker presents the details surrounding the military service of Lieutenant Benefield. Carefully telling his story, the speaker reveals in his development thoughtful insights concerning the factors that made his subject a hero. The events—not merely the language—give the black soldier his claims to emulation. But Professor Cornish makes the speech more than a eulogy to a single man; he presents a splendid tribute to all black soldiers who have "fought for some three hundred years on the front lines of ambiguity." The speaker, perhaps recalling his own experiences in World War II, speaks "with great care" and shows what one observer called "a sensitive feeling for the occasion."

We are come together this peaceful Sunday afternoon to recall the heroism of an American soldier and to dedicate

[1] Delivered at the dedication of the United States Army Reserve Center, Pittsburg, Kansas, November 16, 1975. Title supplied by editor. Quoted by permission.
[2] For biographical note, see Appendix.

this United States Army Reserve Center in his name and to his memory. It is altogether fitting and proper that we should do this. It is a peculiarly American custom to immortalize our heroes and statesmen, our leaders in virtually every walk of life, by casting their names in bronze, or carving them in granite or marble on public buildings, or affixing their names to geographical and political entities like rivers and lakes and cities and especially counties. Better than a dozen Kansas counties are named for Civil War Union generals: Grant, Sheridan, Sherman, Thomas, McPherson, and Scott, to name only half of them. Our own county takes its name from a Civil War colonel, Samuel J. Crawford, who commanded the Second Kansas Colored Volunteer Infantry and became our state's youngest governor. Other counties have been named for Revolutionary War heroes: Montgomery County, for example, for General Richard Montgomery of New York, curiously, rather than for our own James Montgomery of Mound City, colonel of the 34th United States Colored Troops, a more appropriate Montgomery, in my opinion. And there are others named for United States senators, like Stephen A. Douglas of Illinois, Henry Clay of Kentucky, Charles Sumner of Massachusetts, Lewis Linn of Missouri, and even James Henry Lane of Kansas. What we do today is in keeping with established custom, certainly, although there are some important differences which need emphasis. The American soldier whose name we give to this public building today was neither a general nor a colonel, neither a senator nor a cabinet officer, neither a railroad magnate nor a townsite promoter. William M. Benefield Jr., our own hero, was only a second lieutenant; lowliest of the lowly, he held the least admired rank, albeit the most necessary and useful, in the entire military hierarchy.

What, you may ask, what about the enlisted men, the privates and corporals and sergeants, who do the dirtiest work of war? To which one has to respond with other questions: who sees that the enlisted men are fed and clothed and

paid? Who is responsible for the performance of every enlisted man in his unit? Who eats after his men have been
fed, sleeps after he has found shelter for his men? Who but
the second lieutenant, the *good,* the *ideal* second lieutenant,
particularly in an infantry outfit—or in a company of combat engineers? This is to remind you that William M. Benefield Jr. was a second lieutenant in the 77th Engineer Combat Company, attached to the 24th Infantry Regiment, part
of the 25th Division.

To illustrate and emphasize several other significant
points, it is necessary to review Lieutenant Benefield's service
record or, at any rate, an abstract of it which contains the
centrally significant dates in his altogether too brief military
career. He was inducted into the Army of the United States
on September 9, 1944, as World War II was entering its
final stages. On November 13, 1945, a scant two months after
V-J Day, Private Benefield was given an honorable discharge
from the Army of the United States to enable him to enlist,
the next day, in the Regular Army. Slightly over a year later,
Technician Fifth Grade Benefield was demobilized with his
second honorable discharge, this on December 9, 1946. A
month earlier, however, on November 3, 1946, he had joined
the Enlisted Reserve Corps from which he was discharged
honorably on April 29, 1948, this time to enable him to
reenlist in the Regular Army, which he rejoined the following day. Five months later he received another honorable
discharge, his fourth, on October 26, 1948, so that he might,
on the following day, October 27, accept appointment as a
second lieutenant in the Corps of Engineers. His service
record is clear, if you know how to read it: he went from
private AUS to private RA, from private to T/5 to sergeant
to officer candidate to second lieutenant in four years, garner-
ing no less than four honorable discharges en route. After
which, as a lieutenant of combat engineers in the Regular
Army, he eventually shipped out to join US occupation
forces in Japan.

Twenty-five years ago last June the North Koreans moved

south across the 38th parallel of north latitude, an obscure line on an unfamiliar map. That was June 25, 1950. Within three days the North Koreans had captured the South Korean capital of Seoul and were threatening to overrun the entire country.

It is hard to remember today how highly vulnerable the Korean position was twenty-five years ago. Under a tight military budget, the United States did not then have enough men to defend airstrips in Alaska; our major concern was to build up our strength in Europe. When the North Koreans began their full-scale attack, President Harry S. Truman reacted decisively. Fearing a third world war and recalling Manchuria, Ethiopia, and Austria, Truman announced on June 27 that he was sending United States air and naval forces to the aid of South Korea. That same day the United Nations Security Council—with the Russians momentarily absent on a boycott—called on member nations to repel aggression in Korea. President Truman immediately ordered American troops to the battlefront, a rapidly disintegrating battlefront at that. Among the American forces ordered in to stem the tide in early July was the 77th Engineer Combat Company, 24th Infantry Regiment, 25th Division, including our second lieutenant.

Other members of the United Nations, eventually twenty or so, responded to the Security Council appeal and in time sent small contingents to the front. But, as one highly regarded American history has noted, "since the United States sent more than five times as many troops as the rest of the world combined, most Americans regarded the conflict as a US war." For nearly six weeks, the same history records, "North Korean armies advanced down the peninsula driving the smaller South Korean and American forces before them. Fighting desperately, the outnumbered defenders retreated over jagged mountains, across tangled ravines, and through malodorous rice paddies to the southernmost tip of Korea. There they held firm while reinforcements poured into the

port of Pusan from Japan and the United States," and General Douglas MacArthur built up naval and air support.

All this took time, tragically, too much time. There was little naval and air support for the 77th Engineer Combat Company when it met the aggressors in late July. They did the best they could with what they had, in the finest tradition of "poor bloody infantry" and "engineers with hairy ears." Only a month after the North Koreans had taken Seoul, at a place called Sangju, the 77th Engineer Combat Company, fighting a desperate rearguard action and counterattacking the advancing North Koreans, lost a second lieutenant on July 29, 1950.

Lieutenant Benefield played a heroic and tragic role in his first and only campaign, the more tragic because it was a role played, over and over, by earlier unnamed lieutenants leading desperate rear-guard actions in other American wars. While we almost always emerge victorious from our wars, with fully mobilized armed forces and bulging arsenals of all manner of weapons, with millions of men and women in uniform and fleets of ships and planes, all of our wars have caught us ill-prepared or unprepared, with a small regular establishment, an ill-trained militia, and scanty reserve forces. A characteristically peace-loving people, we have largely rejected the old and evil European concept of war as "diplomacy conducted by other means." How many millions of immigrants have come to these American shores to avoid European conscription, from the days of Napoleon I to the 1930s? Consider even our national antipathy to the very words conscription and conscripts. We even refuse to call our conscripts by that name; we prefer, curiously, "draftees." The result is about the same, but apparently we feel better about it. We tend even to blur the distinction between volunteer and drafted recruit: our veterans all volunteered, or at least one gets that impression twenty or so years after the war is over.

Lieutenant Benefield gave his life to buy time, thus join-

ing a goodly company of American soldiers, sailors, and marines through the long years. Lieutenant Benefield was a member of that select fraternity, the Regular Army, a small guard of honor more often the butt of bad jokes than the recipient of national admiration and gratitude. Until another war comes along, and once more the Regulars are caught up, their furloughs canceled, their families broken up overnight. In they go to hold the line, usually an untenable line. The line runs from Lundy's Lane to Fort Sumter, from First Bull Run to San Juan Hill, from Belleau Wood to Pearl Harbor and Bataan. And the Regulars are sent in to hold on long enough to give the nation time to pull up its socks, roll up its sleeves, call up the reserves, build up the fleet, activate and train new regiments and divisions, and settle down to the long, bloody, and expensive work of winning the war. While we honor Lieutenant Benefield, let us remember that he is symbolic and representative of the Regulars in virtually every American war: first to go and, all too often, first to fall.

Lieutenant Benefield is symbolic and representative in several other ways requiring mention today. He is typical of the volunteer American soldier in many respects: a bright and promising young man, vice president of his high school class, caught like hundreds of thousands of his generation (and other American generations before him and after him), caught in the web of war. Typically, he served honorably and well—well enough to win appointment to Officer Candidate School from which he was graduated second in his class, which surprised no one in his home town. Typically, he married his best girl, and typically she followed him to his post of duty in postwar Japan.

There seems to have been nothing out of the ordinary about young Lieutenant Benefield; he was a typical young American soldier beginning a career in the Regular Army. Nothing out of the ordinary except that he died a hero's death in a far-away place we have trouble finding on the map, somewhere on the Naktong River in southeast Korea.

On the recommendation of General MacArthur and by direction of the President, our Lieutenant Benefield was awarded the Distinguished Service Cross "for extraordinary heroism." He was only doing his job, some may say, the dirty and dangerous job of the combat engineer.

That's not all. He was doing more than his job, which is why the citation and the Distinguished Service Cross. Hear this sentence from that citation: "Realizing the danger to personnel of the company, Lieutenant Benefield with complete disregard for his personal safety, went forward alone." He went forward alone to clear a path through an enemy minefield, a job for which he had volunteered. Here was no ordinary young American, no average second lieutenant. Typical? Yes, a typical hero, typical of the best we breed.

Our Lieutenant Benefield is symbolic and representative in one other major way. He served in an Engineer Combat Company attached to the 24th Infantry Regiment, you will recall. And that particular infantry regiment was one of four distinctly different and distinguished regiments, all four authorized by the Congress of the United States in 1866 as recognition of and reward for the battle performance of black soldiers in the armies of the Union during our American Civil War. Those four regiments included the 9th and 10th United States Cavalry, "the Buffalo Soldiers" who compiled a sterling record all over the West in the generation after the Civil War and who saved Teddy Roosevelt's Rough Riders in the fighting around Santiago, Cuba, in July of 1898, and the 24th and 25th United States Infantry. All four regiments established themselves as important and contributing parts of the Regular Army by fighting Indians for twenty-five years after the Civil War and helping to make the West safe for white civilization. Secretary of War Redfield Proctor in his 1889 report called the record of the 24th and 25th Infantry Regiments "excellent" and said of the black soldiers, "They are neat, orderly, obedient, are seldom brought before court-martial, and rarely desert."

These four regiments, the 9th and 10th Cavalry and the

24th and 25th Infantry, were among the only units of the Regular Army open to black enlistment when World War II began. It is significant that Benjamin O. Davis, the first black general in our military history, served in the 9th Cavalry as he made his slow way from lieutenant to brigadier over the span of forty years, from 1901 to 1940. When the Korean War began the 24th Infantry was one of the last racially segregated regiments in the Regular Army. Thanks to some degree at least to the selfless heroism of our Lieutenant Benefield, the armed forces of the United States were racially integrated by President Truman's order long before peace was finally restored to the rugged terrain of Korea. Korea is significant to us as the place where William Benefield gave his life as a member of the armed forces of democracy in mortal combat with Communist aggression. Korea is also significant as the place and occasion for the official death of racial segregation in the armed forces of democracy.

It is hard to remember today how racist American society and institutions were twenty-five years ago. Suffice it to say that we as a nation, as the vaunted leader of the so-called free nations of the world, have come a long way in the past quarter century toward the realization of the proud promises of our national rhetoric. Recall for a moment some significant phrases that go together to compose the American dream: "all men are created equal" and "endowed by their Creator with certain unalienable rights . . . life, liberty, and the pursuit of happiness;" "the land of the free, and the home of the brave," "This nation, under God, shall have a new birth of freedom;" "equal justice under law," and "one nation, under God, indivisible, with liberty and justice for all." We have come a long way toward the realization of these hopes, aspirations, promises, and dreams.

In August of 1968 *Ebony* magazine devoted an entire special issue to the subject of The Black Soldier. Three paragraphs from that special issue deserve our attention today.

A hostage of fate and a warrior against fate, the black soldier has fought for some three hundred years on the front lines of

ambiguity. [*Ambiguity* is defined as "the quality or state of being ambiguous in meaning," and *ambiguous* is defined as "doubtful or uncertain esp. from obscurity or indistinctness."] Never sure of the real identity of *his* enemy or the precise location of *his* battlefield, never completely accepted by his comrades in arms or his white neighbors at home, the black soldier has willingly and repeatedly offered himself as a witness in war to the truths America refuses to recognize in war or peace.

Always, from the first days of the Republic, the black soldier has fought away from home for the freedoms denied him at home. At the back of his mind always has been the vain hope that America would recognize his bravery away from home by recognizing him as a man at home. And in pursuing that hope, the black soldier has written in blood a testament of generosity and gallantry which is a standing reproach and invitation to the Republic.

In every American war, on almost every American battlefield, black men of war have paid in the flesh for the dream denied. And the history of black soldiers and sailors is indelibly etched in the history of the American Republic which lives today because many men, including a long black line of brave black men, marched off to ambiguous graves.

These charges were set down in 1968, remember, written against the background of the assassination of Martin Luther King Jr. and the rioting that scarred scores of American cities immediately thereafter. What we do here today is a partial answer to those charges. What we do here today is partial restitution of that dream denied. What we do here today is thoroughly American in the best sense and meaning. We recognize and honor and memorialize one of our own, a brave young American, whose "extraordinary heroism . . . reflects the highest credit on himself and the military service." We cast his name in bronze, as befits a hero, and we give his name to this Reserve Center as a permanent memorial to him and a lasting reminder to us that he gave the last full measure of devotion in the finest tradition of the United States Army. Second Lieutenant William M. Benefield Jr., Corps of Engineers, has escaped ambiguity: we recognize his bravery away from home by recognizing him as a man at home. He sleeps in an honored grave in Arlington National Cemetery. He will live forever in the hearts of

those who gave him life and of those who knew and loved him. Let his courageous self-sacrifice serve as a model for the citizen-soldiers, officers and men, who use and will use this facility. Let his short life and heroic death serve this entire community as constant reminders that this nation is indeed, and must continue to become, the land of the free as well as the home of the brave.

# APPENDIX

## BIOGRAPHICAL NOTES

BILLINGTON, RAY A. (1903-    ). Born, Bay City, Michigan; Ph.B., University of Wisconsin, 1926; M.A., University of Michigan, 1927; Ph.D., Harvard University, 1933; instructor and assistant professor, Clark University, 1931-37; assistant professor, Smith College, 1937-38; associate professor, 1938-44; professor, 1944; professor, Northwestern University, 1944-49; William Smith Mason Professor of History, 1949-63; senior research associate, Huntington Library, 1963-    ; Harmsworth professor, American History, Oxford University, 1953; Guggenheim Memorial Fellow, 1943-44; lecturer, Johns Hopkins University, 1944; lecturer, University of Cincinnati, 1954; lecturer, University of Kentucky, 1960; president of American Studies Association, 1959-63; Phi Beta Kappa Associate; Sigma Delta Chi; author, *The Protestant Crusade*, 1938; *Westward Expansion*, 1949; *American History Since 1865*, 1950; *The Far Western Frontier, 1830-1860*, 1956; *America's Frontier Heritage*, 1960; *Genesis of Frontier Thesis*, 1971; *Frederick Jackson Turner*, 1973; author and co-author of numerous other books and journal articles.

CHURCH, FRANK (1924-    ). Born, Boise, Idaho; on debating team, Boise high school; B.A., Stanford University, 1947; LL.B., 1950; admitted to Idaho bar, 1950; practiced law in Boise, 1950-56; Idaho chairman, Crusade for Freedom, 1954, 1955; keynote speaker, state Democratic convention, 1952; member, US Senate (Democrat, Idaho), 1957-    ; member, Senate Committee on Foreign Relations; Senate Committee on Interior and Insular Affairs; Senate Special Committee on Aging; chairman, Senate Select Committee on Intelligence; keynote speaker, Democratic National Convention, 1960; US Army, World War II; elected one of Ten Outstanding Young Men of 1957, US Junior Chamber of Commerce; recipient, American Legion Oratorical Contest Award, 1941 ("The American Way of Life"); Joffre Debate Medal, Stanford University, 1947; member, Phi Beta Kappa. (See also *Current Biography: March 1958.*)

CORNISH, DUDLEY T. (1915-    ). Born, Carmel, New York; B.A., University of Rochester, 1938; M.A., University of Colorado, 1947; Ph.D., 1949; assistant professor, then associate professor, Kansas State College of Pittsburg, 1949-58; professor of history, 1958-    ; chairman, department of social science, 1959-61; department of history, 1966-    ; US Army, 1942-46; author *The Sable Arm: Negro*

217

*Troops in the Union Army, 1861-1865,* 1966; editor in chief, *Midwest Quarterly,* 1959-67; associate editor, 1967-  ; president, Kansas Historical Society, 1973-74.

EVERHEART, WILLIAM E. (1916-  ). Born, Pottsboro, Texas; B.A., Trinity University, 1937; Th.M., Princeton University, 1940; ordained to ministry United Presbyterian Church, 1940; minister, Westminster Presbyterian Church, Amarillo, Texas, 1951-62; senior minister, First and Calvary Church, Springfield, Missouri, 1962-71; president, Drury College, 1971-  ; USNR, 1942-45; member, Blue Key, Omicron Delta Kappa, Pi Kappa Delta.

FORD, GERALD R (UDOLPH) (1913-  ). Born, Omaha, Nebraska; B.A., University of Michigan, 1935; LL.B., Yale Law School, 1941; admitted Michigan bar, 1941; private law practice, Grand Rapids, Michigan, 1941-49; member, US House of Representatives (Republican, Michigan), 1949-73; minority leader, 1965-73; appointed Vice President by President Nixon, confirmed by Congress, December 6, 1973; became President upon resignation of Nixon, August 9, 1974; USN, 1942-46. (See also *Current Biography: November 1975.*)

GALBRAITH, JOHN KENNETH (1908-  ). Born, near Iona Station, Ontario, Canada; B.S., University of Toronto, 1931; M.S., University of California, 1933; Ph.D., 1934; numerous honorary degrees from American and foreign universities; naturalized, 1937; instructor, Harvard University, 1934-39; assistant professor of economics, Princeton University, 1939-42; professor of economics, Harvard University, 1949-59; Paul M. Warburg Professor of Economics, 1959-60, 1963-75; deputy administrator, OPA, 1941-42; director, US Strategic Bombing Survey, 1945; member, board of editors, *Fortune Magazine,* 1943-48; US ambassador to India, 1961-63; adviser to Adlai Stevenson, 1952, 1956 and to John F. Kennedy in 1960; author, *American Capitalism,* 1952, 1955; *Economics and the Art of Controversy,* 1954; *The Great Crash, 1929,* (revised) 1955; *The Affluent Society,* 1958, (2d ed.) 1969, (3d ed. revised) 1976; *The Liberal Hour,* 1960; *The McLandress Dimension,* 1962; *Economic Development,* 1964; *The Scotch,* 1964; *The New Industrial State,* 1967, (2d revised ed.) 1971; *The Triumph,* 1968; *Indian Painting: The Scene, Themes and Legends,* 1968; *Ambassador's Journal: A Personal Account of the Kennedy Years,* 1969; *Economics, Peace and Laughter,* 1971; *A China Passage,* 1973; and *Money: Whence It Came, Where It Went,* 1975. (See also *Current Biography: May 1975.*)

GRAHAM, BILLY (WILLIAM FRANKLIN) (1918-  ). Born, Charlotte, North Carolina; Th.B., Florida Bible Seminary, Tampa, Florida, 1940; B.A., Wheaton College, 1943; honorary degrees,

Houghton College, Baylor University, The Citadel, William Jewell College; ordained to ministry, Southern Baptist Convention, 1939; minister, First Baptist Church, Western Springs, Illinois, 1943-45; evangelist 1944-  ; first vice president, Youth for Christ, 1945-48; president, Northwestern College, Minneapolis, 1947-52; founder and president, Billy Graham Evangelistic Association, 1963-  ; editor, *Decision Magazine*, United Bible Society, 1963-  ; weekly speaker, Hour of Decision radio program, ABC, NBC, Mutual networks, 1950-  ; numerous trips to Europe and Asia, preached in nearly every country of the world; author of *Calling Youth to Christ*, 1947; *Revival in Our Times*, 1950; *America's Hour of Decision*, 1951; *Korean Diary*, 1953; *Peace With God*, 1953; *Peace Aflame*, 1965; *The Challenge*, 1969; *The Jesus Generation*, 1971. (See also *Current Biography: January 1973*.)

HOWARD, JOHN A. (1921-  ). Born, Winnetka, Illinois; B.S., Northwestern University, 1947; M.A., 1949; Ph.D., 1962; instructor of French, Palos Verdes College, Rolling Hills, California, 1947-49; dean of students, 1949-51; vice president, 1950-51; president, 1951-55; president, Rockford (Illinois) College, 1960-  ; president, American Association of Presidents of Independent Colleges and Universities, 1969-72; executive vice chairman, President's Committee on Government Contracts, 1956-57; member, US Task Force on Higher Education, 1969-70; US Commission on Marijuana and Drug Abuse, 1971-73; National Council of Scholars, 1969-70; US Army, 1942-45; Silver Star with Oakleaf Cluster, Purple Heart with Oakleaf Cluster; recipient, Horatio Alger Award, 1967.

JORDAN, VERNON E. JR. (1935-  ). Born, Atlanta, Georgia; B.A., DePauw University, 1957; first prize, Indiana Interstate Oratorical Contest, sophomore year; LL.D., Howard University, 1960; circuit vice president of American Law Students Association while at Howard University; helped to desegregate the University of Georgia; clerk in law office of civil rights attorney Donald Hollowell; field secretary, NAACP, Georgia branch, 1962; set up law partnership in Arkansas with another civil rights lawyer, Wiley A. Barnton, 1964; director, Voter Education Project for the Southern Regional Council, 1964-68; executive director, United Negro College Fund, 1970-72; director, National Urban League, January 1972-  ; member, Arkansas and Georgia bar associations; US Supreme Court bar; American Bar Association; Common Cause; Rockefeller Foundation; Twentieth Century Fund; other service organizations; has held fellowships at Harvard University's Institute of Politics, the John F. Kennedy School of Government, and the Metropolitan Applied Research Center. (See also *Current Biography: February 1972*.)

KELLEY, CLARENCE M. (1911- ). Born, Kansas City, Missouri; B.A., University of Kansas, 1936; LL.B., University of Missouri—Kansas City, 1940; served the Federal Bureau of Investigation in ten cities including Pittsburgh, Des Moines, Kansas City, Washington, Houston, Seattle, and San Francisco, 1940-44, 1946-61; chief of police, Kansas City, Missouri, 1961-73; director, FBI, 1973- ; USNR, 1944-46. (See also *Current Biography: May 1974.*)

KISSINGER, HENRY ALFRED (1923- ). Born, Fürth, Germany; B.A., summa cum laude, Harvard, 1950; M.A., 1952; Ph.D., 1954; arrived, United States, 1938; naturalized, 1943; executive director, Harvard International Seminar, 1951-60; lecturer, government, Harvard University, 1957-59; associate professor, 1959-62; professor, 1962-69; director, special studies project, Rockefeller Brothers Fund, Inc., 1956-59; consultant to Presidents Eisenhower, Kennedy, Johnson; assistant to President, for national security affairs, 1969- ; secretary, US Department of State, 1973- ; US Army, 1943-46; recipient, Bronze Star; member, Phi Beta Kappa; author, *Nuclear Weapons and Foreign Policy*, 1957; *A World Restored*, 1957; *The Necessity For Choice: Prospects of American Foreign Policy*, 1961; *The Troubled Partnership: A Reappraisal of the Atlantic Alliance*, 1965; *American Foreign Policy: Three Essays*, 1969; over forty articles in various journals. (See also *Current Biography: June 1972.*)

KRUG, JUDITH F. (1940- ). Born, Pittsburgh, Pennsylvania; B.A., University of Pittsburgh, 1961; M.A., University of Chicago, 1964; assistant librarian, downtown center, University of Chicago, 1961-62; reference librarian, John Crerar Library, Chicago, 1962-63; cataloger, Northwestern University Dental School, Chicago, 1963-65; research analyst, American Library Association, Chicago, 1965-67; director, Office for Intellectual Freedom, American Library Association, 1967- ; member, Phi Beta Kappa, Beta Phi Mu, Pi Sigma Alpha, Delta Sigma Rho; co-editor, *Newsletter on Intellectual Freedom*, 1970- ; and Freedom to Read Foundation *News*, 1972- ; numerous articles in library and educational journals.

MARCUS, STANLEY (1905- ). Born, Dallas, Texas; B.A., Harvard University, 1925; honorary degree, D. Humanities, Southern Methodist University, 1965; associated with Neiman Marcus, Dallas, 1926- ; executive vice president, 1935-50; president, 1950-72; chairman of board, chief executive officer, 1972- ; chairman of executive committee, 1975- ; vice president, Carter Hawley Hale Stores, Inc., Los Angeles, California; director, Republic of Texas Corp., New York Life Insurance Co., numerous civic and educa-

tional organizations; author, *Mind the Store*, 1974; articles in *Fortune, Atlantic Monthly, Look, Pageant, Glamour,* and *Saturday Evening Post.*

MOYNIHAN, DANIEL P. (1927-    ). Born, Tulsa, Oklahoma; B.A., Tufts University, cum laude, 1948; M.A., 1949; Ph.D., Fletcher School of Law and Diplomacy, 1961; LL.D., St. Louis University, 1968; Fulbright fellow, London (England) School of Economics and Political Science, 1950-51; special assistant to US Secretary of Labor, 1961-62; executive assistant, 1962-63; Assistant Secretary of Labor, 1963-65; director, Joint Center Urban Studies, Massachusetts Institute of Technology and Harvard University, 1966-69; professor, education and urban politics, senior member, Kennedy School of Government, Harvard University, 1966-73; assistant for urban affairs to President of United States, 1969-70; counselor to President Nixon, member of cabinet, 1971-73; US ambassador to India, 1973-74; US ambassador to United Nations, 1975-76; USNR, 1944-47; member, American Academy of Arts and Sciences; numerous committees, including New York State Democratic Convention, 1958-60; member, New York state delegation, Democratic National Convention, 1960; vice chairman, Woodrow Wilson International Center for Scholars, 1971-    ; author, *Maximum Feasible Misunderstanding,* 1969; *Beyond the Melting Pot* (with Nathan Glazer), 1963. (See also *Current Biography: February 1968.*)

PARSON, MARY JEAN (1934-    ). Born, Houston, Texas; B.A., Birmingham Southern College, 1956; M.F.A., Yale University, 1959; director, special projects, ANTA, 1959-60; producer, "The Sap of Life," off-Broadway, 1961; business manager, Mineola Playhouse, 1962; assistant to president, National Performing Arts, 1963; director of production exhibits, Better Living Center, New York World's Fair, 1964-65; associated with American Broadcasting Company, 1965-    ; director, planning, development and administration, ABC Leisure Group II, 1975-    ; member, Phi Beta Kappa, Mortar Board, Alpha Psi Omega.

SAWHILL, JOHN C. (1936-    ). Born, Cleveland, Ohio; B.A., cum laude, Princeton University, 1958; Ph.D., New York University, 1963; with Merrill, Lynch, Pierce, Fenner & Smith, 1958-60; associate dean, professor, School of Business Administration, New York University, 1960-63; director, credit research and planning, Commercial Credit Company, Baltimore, 1963-65; senior vice president, 1968-73; associate director, US Office of Management and Budget, 1973-74; Federal Energy Administrator, April-October, 1974; president, New York University, September 1, 1975-    .

# CUMULATIVE AUTHOR INDEX

### 1970-1971—1975-1976

A cumulative author index to the volumes of REPRESENTATIVE AMERICAN SPEECHES for the years 1937-1938 through 1959-1960 appears in the 1959-1960 volume and for the years 1960-1961 through 1969-1970 in the 1969-1970 volume.